Training to Win

Strategies for Today's Industrial Challenges

Training to Win

Strategies for Today's Industrial Challenges

Jay M. Orlin

Nichols Publishing
New York

Books bearing the Nichols Publishing imprint are published by GP Publishing, Inc.

Library of Congress Cataloging-in-Publication Data

Orlin, Jay M., 1943-
Training to win : strategies for today's industrial challenges
Jay M. Orlin.
p. cm.
Bibliography: p.
ISBN 0-89397-323-8
1. Employees, Training of—United States. 2. Occupational training—United States. 3. Competition, International. I. Title.
HF5549.5.T7075 1987 88-11378
658.3'124—dc19 CIP

Printed and bound in the United States of America
94 93 92 91 90 89 88 5 4 3 2 1

To Rose, An American Beauty
Thanks, Mom, for the confidence

To Paula, Queen of Hearts and Flowers
Thanks for your generous support

Acknowledgments

This book derives from the expertise of many people. I have been fortunate to have received information, encouragement, key referrals, proofreading, editing, advice, and many other contributions to this book. I give my sincere thanks and appreciation to those named below:

Russ Anderson, Senior Project Manager, Nuclear Regulatory Commission Technical Training Center
Dr. Robert Behm, Dean of Distant Learning, San Diego State University
Dr. John Crosby, Vice President, LSI Operations, Western Digital Corp.
Robert Danna, Director, Engineering Services, General Physics Corp.
Michael Dawson, Program Development Manager, General Physics Corp.
Robert Deutsch, President, RWD Technologies
Ron Epps, Manager, Mission Training, NASA, Houston
Joanne L. Erickson, Editor
Dr. Paul Elliott, RWD Technologies
Michael Ettl, Director, Technical Training, General Electric, BWR
Frank Frediani, Systems Technician, Northern Telecom
Arthur Fleming, Literary Agent
William Harding, Senior Design Engineer, Northern Telecom
John Lawrence, Manager, Public Relations, NASA, Houston
James Leahy, Dean, Navy Technical Training Program
Diane Loder, Administrative Specialist, Northern Telecom
Paul Lorenz, Vice-President, Marketing, Courseware, Inc.
Jim Macek, Corporate Manager for Automation and Computer-Integrated Manufacturing, AMD Corp.

Roger Maude, Technical Staff, Northern Telecom
Captain James McGarvie, Director, Flight Training, PSA
Steven Nesbitt, Deputy Chief, Media Services Branch, NASA, Houston
Mike Norman, Manager, Productivity Methods and Systems, Northern Telecom
Jeff Oberlin, Manager, Planning and Evaluation, Training and Education Department, Motorola, Inc.
Paula Orlin, Manager, Home Support Systems
Thomas Orton, President, Integrated Semiconductor Training, Inc.
Dolf Payer, Skills Training Systems
Ralph Pettit, Senior Staff Specialist, Cubic Defense Systems
Cora Pendergast, Manager, Instructional Design, Northern Telecom
Kenneth Rebeck, RWD Technologies
Douglas Runnels, Training Consultant
Fred Ward, Owner, North County Systems

Contents

Introduction

Almost any discussion of U.S. competitiveness in the international market place includes thoughts on the productivity and quality of the American worker. The relative strength of the dollar and other economic conditions contribute to our competitiveness but do not, in themselves, determine productivity and quality. However, management decisions at every level in a corporation directly influence them.

I hope this book will demystify technical training for those managers who may face decisions about it. Better management decisions about the role of technical training in corporations today and in the future require a better understanding of it. By improving our technical training efforts we can strengthen our quality and productivity. I have tried to cover everything a manager who is not a training specialist needs to know.

Effective management is vital for corporations to carry out their business plans. It would appear, from the countless dollars spent on management training every year, that most people agree. One major role of management is to ensure that workers have the tools and knowledge to perform their jobs. This book will benefit such an effort.

Any effective strategy for improving the performance of U.S. companies must include a well-planned technical training component. Managers at all levels need to appreciate its importance. Designing and delivering training is time consuming and requires considerable effort and cannot be accomplished without commitment from all levels of management.

Japan's educational system features much more emphasis on achievement in mathematics and science than does education in our country. This gives Japanese industries a more technically oriented pool of workers. Management enhances that base with extensive technical training, resulting in the high quality and productivity of Japanese industries today.

U.S. industry must respond proactively to this situation. Our industrial training technologies are probably the best in the world and certainly outstrip those of the Japanese. We should take advantage of this asset by building strategies that deliver continual improvements in productivity. We must adopt the long-term view of technical training when developing our work force. To regain world industrial supremacy, we must match our competitors in intensity and foresight and beat them with superior skills on the factory floors.

Industries of the future will need ever-increasing numbers of technical workers in their factories. In fact, it appears that all jobs will have more and more technical components. Therefore, we must begin now to improve our technical training programs, and in this book I try to show how managers can go about doing that. After reading the volume, the reader will know all the elements that make a training program successful, and how to develop a top-notch one. I reveal many lessons we can learn from the Japanese on how to utilize technical training to ensure high levels of worker competence. I also give examples of some of the best technical training programs in the country, and I mention several resources and services available to people involved in technical training. My discussion should help managers ask the right questions and look in the right places to develop high-quality training programs for their employees.

This information comes largely from my experience, first-hand interviews with technical trainers in many industries, and literature. I have also included anecdotes and profiles of some interesting training companies.

In *Training to Win,* I hope to provide information, insight, and guidelines that will be useful to anyone interested in high-quality training. I have, therefore, included both exotic and everyday training applications: my examples of training range from astronauts to factory operators. Although this book emphasizes high-tech industries, its principles apply to any setting.

1

The Ultimate Competitive Advantage

Winning in business does not differ fundamentally from winning at anything else. The world of sports rests on the notion of competition. It has elaborate rules and procedures used to determine who wins a game and who wins a championship. Athletes work extremely hard preparing to compete for the honors and rewards of winning. Unless a competitor has extraordinary natural talent, it is the training that makes the difference.

Who wins Olympic medals? Usually, people who have not only committed themselves to the effort but have also had the benefit of excellent training. When a team of talented individuals fails miserably, people often blame the coach. Both owners and the public hold coaches accountable for the success of a team. Implicit in that accountability is the expectation that they will maximize team resources to put in a winning performance.

Boards of directors and stockholders have exactly the same expectation of their CEOs and presidents: that they maximize team resources and put in a winning performance. In sports, "winning" means a championship title or at least a good crack at it. In business, it is achievement of the goals of the company. In both cases the "score" tells how well the team accomplishes its goals.

The chief indicators of a company's success are financial, although strategic components figure in as well. Financial indicators, often referred to as "the bottom line," are profitability, growth in net assets, payment to shareholders, and other measures involving money. Stragegic indicators include such considerations as technological breakthroughs, improved market shares, and acquisitions that strengthen the company.

With a viable product line and reasonable trade conditions, companies achieve positive indicators when workers are well-trained and motivated to succeed. The key resource to maximize is the human resource. There is no excuse for cutting corners in the training of people because the market place doesn't listen. It simply judges and buys the best products for the best price.

A company's ultimate competitive advantage is its ability to train and retrain people effectively. Consider, for example, the approach the Japanese have taken when establishing an auto factory in another country. They came to the United States, opened factories, and achieved high quality and productivity by investing in training their employees. In some cases the entire senior and middle management teams were sent to Japan for several weeks to learn about the company and its philosophies. Success has not come from superhuman Japanese workers or lower Japanese pay scales. Their factories are populated by the same American auto workers who built Fords and Pontiacs before they learned how to build Toyotas and Hondas. Success has come from *training*.

Dr. James Belasco, a professor of management at San Diego State University and management consultant to IBM, Royal Dutch Airlines, Shell, and McDonnell Douglas, has pointed out that when Nissan built a small truck plant in Smyrna, Tennessee, it spent an unprecedented $40,000 per employee for training before ever opening its doors. In addition to technical training, the company taught quality control methods, statistics, and teamwork. The result? Nissan recouped its training investment in the first nine months of operation (Belasco, 1987). The plant has been frequently singled out as the most productive and efficient automobile factory in the world.

Thus, a well-planned training strategy can help create a winning organization. The goals of the business plan must be the driving force behind the training plans. Experienced training managers should be very familiar with the goals and strategies in the business and operating plans of their companies. The training manager has a proactive role to play in the organization. That role includes discovering opportunities in which training can clearly and decisively influence performance.

To build a strategy, top management must be involved, especially for two critical reasons: time and money. First, consider time. The top managers must be committed to training themselves in order to understand the company's direction for its training strategy. They must also comprehend what the initial training effort is likely to cost the organization in terms of output capacity. They must adjust their expectations and not overcommit the organization. If schedules are too aggressive, most of the training will be preempted by output demands—i.e., by "fire fighting." Managers who understand the strategic plan can hold on to the course during times of pressure and realize long-term benefits.

Now consider money. To start up a quality training effort, one must be prepared to spend some money. Costs may arise from internal staffing, outside consulting, purchase of equipment, development of materials, or other necessities. Managers must analyze these costs from an educated perspective. They must understand what is being spent and why. As with any expenditure in business, there should be an expectation of payback somewhere down the line. Management also has to ride out any temporary loss of productivity in favor of the long-range benefits of training.

The ultimate competitive advantage—the ability to train and retrain people effectively—comes about only when actively supported by an informed management team. After all, a manager's role includes creating all possible conditions to ensure that employees succeed.

When the importance of training becomes an integral part of company culture, spin-off benefits result. For example, when a new product or process goes on line in a factory, employees expect a thorough training program for it. They are not apt to accept hurried or inadequate instruction. This kind of pushback is healthy: it puts responsibility back where it belongs—on the team introducing the new product or process. The team's work is not done until it has ensured that proper training accompanies the introduction.

Another advantage of having the means for such training is the ability to respond effectively to unexpected conditions. Crises such as a business downturn or a competitor hiring away experienced employees require rapid response in terms of retraining. Experienced training and quality training materials come to the fore under such conditions.

Another plus: along with the development of technical training programs comes some valuable documentation, derived in part from expert employees. In time, some of those experts will leave the company, but the training materials they leave behind will preserve some of that expertise. This is no trivial benefit because departing experts often have specialized knowledge few other people have.

It all comes back to competitive advantage. In most businesses, everyone can purchase equipment from the same vendors and pay similar amounts for it. It's difficult to make a living from proprietary technologies because the rate of knowledge explosion makes that base unstable. It is the skill of the employees that wins the day. The hands that touch the product, the fingers that enter the data, the minds that solve the problems—training *these* gives a company—and nation—its ultimate competitive advantage.

2

The Worker of the Future

The workers of today often find themselves operating advanced and expensive equipment. In all high-tech industries, equipment costs are staggering. Technological breakthroughs can, and do, make obsolete millions of dollars' worth of equipment every year. The new models are inevitably more complex and more expensive than their predecessors. Because manufacturers cannot afford to be left behind in the capabilities race, they must continually upgrade. The price tag can easily run into hundreds of thousands of dollars for a single piece of equipment.

Almost all jobs in the high-tech factory of the future will have an extensive technical component. Increased sophistication of equipment will require more specialization by technicians and more time devoted to each piece of equipment. Engineering professionals will be asked to spend more and more of their time on improving processes. They will be less available to make repairs, troubleshoot, or inspect for quality. Therefore, it will become more important for people on the line to think for themselves and troubleshoot on a daily basis.

Simultaneously applying different engineering practices can greatly enhance new product start-ups. In "concurrent engineering," both product engineers and process engineers work together from the beginning of product design. Although this approach may sound perfectly logical, at present companies rarely use it. At most firms, engineers responsible for designing products are only minimally acquainted with the details of the manufacturing. Sometimes, the designer works hundreds of miles away from the manufacturing site. Bringing product and process engineers together can ensure that the product is designed with manufacturability in mind.

Design for manufacturability and concurrent engineering are useful strategies that can decrease the risk of creating a product that is incompatible with factory conditions. This approach could be taken a step further by including *human performance experts* on the design team as well. Even when product characteristics fit factory configurations, there is still the challenge of transferring the technology, which requires a thorough analysis of how the work has to be done.

In one case, an automobile factory upgraded significantly with more robots and automation, yet its existing job classifications had no relevance to the new style of manufacture. The new technology required new technical skills and knowledge, which in turn required new job descriptions and, in fact, a renegotiation of job classifications with the union. Not surprisingly, the personnel snags hindered the technology start-up. The loss of time could have been averted had the right human performance specialists been involved in the planning.

Another important reason to expand the team involves technical training. New equipment, such as robots or automated work stations, must be *maintained.* If the maintenance technicians are not well-trained on the equipment, serious problems can arise. The same applies to operator training, which is time consuming if done correctly and needs to be planned well ahead of implementation.

Equipment operators in a factory or office must learn a complex set of skills. Some of the jobs in a high-tech factory take 3-6 months to learn completely, while others can be mastered in a couple of weeks. Most of the labor in a high-tech factory is done by operators, semiskilled people trained to do the jobs using intensely expensive equipment. In most manufacturing plants, operators and skilled tradespeople are the primary target of inhouse training departments. Yet most training dollars are spent on *management* training.

The movement toward automation indicates there will be increased reliance on computers. In manufacturing today, computers tend to control the discrete piece of equipment into which they are built. With automation, the computer becomes responsible not only for performing a job but also for the inspection and movement of work in a factory. Much of the sensitive decision making will be done by computers. For example, today most factories producing electronics devote significant portions of their labor to inspections of work processes. This procedure is used whether the process is human or mechanical. Equipment available today has the ability to search for defects and make decisions about quality.

If you look 5-15 years into the future, you can easily imagine "lights-out factories"—ones at which everything is done by automation so that lighting is not required full time to aid the human eye—in every developed country. Inside the dimly lit, humming cleanrooms, material moves from work station to work station. Raw material is pulled from inventory supplies as needed, and moves in correct sequence from operation to operation. Yield and throughput performance are monitored. White-coated technicians and managers study the readouts and intervene if necessary.

What makes this giant, humming machine called an "automated factory" work? Highly trained people, a few operators and skilled tradespeople, many computer experts, even more equipment experts, and a few managers. A good everyday analogy is Disney World. On the surface everything is clean, life seems simple and idyllic, events occur right on time. Below the surface, however, is a beehive bustling with activity. Everything is carefully timed and maintained so that the hive hums. Disney World thrives because, among other things, its managers are meticulous about training.

Automated factories fall into two basic categories: hard automation and flexible automation. By understanding the difference, one can appreciate the magnitude of difficulty associated with the most advanced lights-out factories.

The term *hard automation* describes a dedicated manufacturing line or factory in which the output is a single product line with minimal variations. In essence, the purpose is to arrange the equipment and work flow in such a manner that raw material is fed into the beginning of the line and a high-quality, reliable product emerges at the end. This type of manufacturing is financially possible only when there is sufficient demand for the specific product the dedicated facility will produce.

Major benefits of hard automation include the elimination of frequent calibration and setting changes on equipment, and the ability to install robots and inspection equipment that continually use the same specifications and criteria. These features result in significantly faster throughput times for products and much higher unit-to-start yields.

The downside of hard automation is expense and lack of flexibility. As mentioned earlier, high-tech manufacturing requires equipment upgrading that is ever more expensive. When equipment and buildings are dedicated to one product line, they are often unsuitable for a new product. When the cost curve on a product goes down—that is, when competition forces the prices down—the hard automation factory faces increasing pressure. Lacking flexibility, it must continue to run its product or shut down to retool. Consequently, the company may have to operate at a loss for a long time, or close its doors permanently.

The Mitsubishi semiconductor plant in Saijo, Japan, exemplifies hard automation. With two fully automated, in-line, serial-flow manufacturing lines, it produces two different density semiconductors. It needs higher-than-average equipment uptime to be successful and, for this reason, must instantly attend to any equipment failure. This requires maintaining a high technician head count—much higher, one would imagine, than originally projected when the factory was built. This pushes costs up. On the other hand, the plant has achieved world-record yields, with final outs in excess of 75 percent (a cumulative yield number requiring successive factory, assembly, and test yields in the mid to high 90s).

The dedication of manufacturing lines contributes significantly to high yields in that factory because it greatly reduces the handling of production equipment and materials. In semiconductor manufacturing, quartz plates with microscopic images on them (photomasks) are used to project patterns onto wafers. These determine what the product will be. In the standard factory, the equipment that does the projection is used for every product. It may be required to change the photomasks in a piece of equipment 8-12 times in a 24-hour period, to accommodate the variety of products required by the schedule. This repeated handling makes the masks vulnerable to deterioration even when the greatest care is taken. It also makes the equipment continually susceptible to minor destabilization of settings. In the dedicated line, however, the mask is inserted and not removed, except for scheduled cleaning and inspections, unless it develops a problem (a rare occurrence).

Flexible automation refers to the factory or manufacturing line designed to adapt easily to changes in products and to utilize the same piece of equipment for many levels of production. The sophisticated requirements of the computer control systems, coupled with robotics and automation issues, make flexible automation a much more difficult proposition. Operations at a quiet, lights-out factory fall into the category of flexible automation.

Matsushita Industrial Corporation is a leader in the development of the factory of the future. Together with Yokogawa Hewlett Packard (YHP), Matsushita built a fully flexible, integrated circuit manufacturing plant in northern Japan in 1986. The factory is, at this point, an experimental lab for the corporation. Although intended to produce significant volume and superior products, it is not, at this point, as cost effective as the factories of the future will be. To function at full capacity, the factory must maintain a high head count and redundant systems for which there is a perceived vulnerability. Matsushita is committed to making the concept work.

In addition to the layout and design of the factory, Matsushita designs and builds some of its own manufacturing equipment. Its proprietary inhouse equipment has some unique advantages. For example, its own wire bonding equipment handles twice as many units twice as fast as does anything else on the market. The corporation has made similar innovations in other areas.

The secrets of advanced manufacturing technologies are usually kept under wraps in Japan. The semiconductor example discussed above has its limitations. For instance, although Matsushita provides a good illustration of my points, it is still regarded as a second-tier electronics company in Japan. The first-tier companies (NEC, Toshiba, Fujitsu, Hitachi) maintain strict security for their advanced manufacturing techniques and reveal information selectively.

U.S. companies working aggressively in the semiconductor field include IBM, Texas Instruments, Intel, and National Semiconductor. IBM reportedly spent over a billion dollars in 1985 on an automation program. It is committed to advanced manufacturing as a key element of its business strategy and will undoubtedly remain on the leading edge. Intel and Texas Instruments have committed to strategies for flexible manufacturing. National Semiconductor and Digital Equipment Corporation have collaborated on the Odyssey Project in Santa Clara, California, which focuses on assembly.

An exceedingly constructive development in the competition for producing advanced semiconductor manufacturing technologies is Sematech, a consortium of semiconductor producers that was established May 1987 to conduct research germane to manufacturing in the semiconductor industry. Sematech will eventually provide its member companies with knowledge that will enable them to assert world leadership in semiconductor manufacturing technology.

The consortium has built a fabrication and research facility in Austin, Texas, and expects to begin processing silicon wafers by late 1988. It has committed to a three-phase approach in its research: one, the demonstration of basic manufacturing capability; two, achieving performance that matches the world's best; and three, helping members become world leaders in semiconductor manufacturing.

In addition to on-site research, Sematech has initiated a "Centers for Excellence" program. The program brings selected universities with expertise in semiconductor manufacturing together with researchers and manufacturers. Research at the universities will be funded through Sematech.

Sematech is funded half by the U.S. government and half by its member companies. Its operating expenses will be approximately $250 million per year, and the effort is ultimately expected to cost approximately $1.5 billion. Member companies include Advanced Micro Devices, AT&T, Digital Equipment, Harris, Hewlett-Packard, Intel, IBM, LSI Logic, Micron Technology, Motorola, National Semiconductor, Rockwell International, and Texas Instruments. Membership in the consortium is open to other U.S. semiconductor companies.

In January 1988, Sematech received a significant boost in credibility and prestige when IBM and AT&T announced they were transferring their most advanced, state-of-the-art technologies to the consortium. IBM contributed a four-megabit DRAM and AT&T contributed a 64-kilobit SRAM, which utilizes 0.7 micron geometries. The acquisition of these demonstration vehicles gives Sematech a running start on its ambitious goals. It will use these products to expedite the completion of Phase Two, which, among other things, targets the successful manufacture of 0.5 micron devices.

Sematech performs research under conditions that closely approximate the conditions of an actual manufacturing environment. The goal is to transfer pragmatic information that can be applied quickly by the member companies, as opposed to pure research.

One of the most advanced European companies in flexible manufacturing is Philips International B.V. In its Eindhover National Laboratories, the Dutch company is reportedly doing some breakthrough, state-of-the-art work in advanced manufacturing technologies.

General Motors has made a massive commitment to automated, flexible manufacturing. It has spent an estimated $40 billion during the 1980s upgrading and building new modern manufacturing facilities. It has also made selective acquisitions of technical engineering, research, and robotics companies, which will enhance its efforts.

The firm's most advanced project to date is Saginaw-Vanguard. The Saginaw division, working with maximum support from the corporate advanced engineering staff, completed a prototype of a factory of the future in late 1987. The factory produces transaxles for front-wheel drive vehicles. Staffed by a small, highly technical work force, it operates in about 70,000 square feet. The work is all coordinated and monitored from a control room with computer displays and digital indicators.

In addition to functioning as a prototype, the factory builds parts as needed, to order, for replacement on vehicles now on the road. The factory's quick turn-around on filling orders for the parts eliminates the need to maintain a large inventory.

The product is sophisticated from the standpoint of precise machining and exacting assembly requirements. With the input of castings and extruded parts, the factory goes into operation and completes a highly machined, high-tolerance transaxle. The line is built with great flexibility in mind. It is capable of building transaxles of different specifications if necessary.

Saginaw-Vanguard is an example of factory-level control. Not only does each cell complete a process without human intervention, but the cells interact with one another, completing the entire manufacturing process independently of human operators. The firm relies on sophisticated maintenance practices to ensure successful plant operation.

Another GM division, Allison Gas Turbines, is an example of cell-level control. A manufacturer of high-performance helicopter motors, it is highly automated as well. The plant is designed for automation at the cell-only level. GM designed the work flow so that cells operate in a completely automated fashion but do not interface with one another.

GM is striving to maximize the transfer of lessons learned and new technologies developed through a technology transfer group, which collects and organizes knowledge gained from divisions such as Allison Gas Turbines and Saginaw-Vanguard.

The point here is not who is ahead of whom in the race today, but the inescapable reality that increasing sophistication and technical training are essential for workers in companies that aspire to succeed in the market place.

The worker of the future will have to be more technically oriented. Many jobs will have changed from semiskilled to skilled. The increase in the need for technicians will be dramatic. A factor that will become even more critical in the automated factory will be equipment uptime because an automated factory is staffed with a much smaller complement of operators than is found in a typical factory today. In the event of a manufacturing emergency, there will not be enough operators available to work around the problems. For example, in the typical factory today, there are enough skilled people working on the line to allow some of them to pitch in during a crisis, do extra shifts, or work more than one station. There are ways to stretch the human resources. Machines, however, function at finite levels and in finite ways, making it difficult to be creative when a key component of the system goes down. Therefore, downtime will be more costly. Central computer failures will generally be handled by a redundant backup computer, but there is still increased vulnerability.

The demand for specialists in equipment, computer troubleshooting, robotics, and software designers has already exceeded the supply in this nation. That demand will increase tremendously in the upcoming decades. The U.S. Bureau of

Labor projects a 330-percent increase in all types of technicians between 1985 and 2000. Industry, the military, and educational institutions will be competing for those resources. They will each strive to become more competitive as employers, and industry will have to struggle all the more for resources.

One outcome will be more inhouse training programs. Companies will have to provide more and higher-quality training for their technicians, both to support the business and to attract the best people. They will also have to be much more careful in training the first-line operators because those jobs will keep changing to incorporate more technical skills. Such changes are already underway in the high-tech factories: more companies are redefining the basic labor job to include a more technical component. Operators who have traditionally been trained only to run equipment or do inspections are now getting the opportunity to learn and exercise new skills.

The high demand for equipment maintenance specialists requires managers to devise new ways to keep everything running. They look at their large labor pool and ask, "Can we teach the operators some basics about how their equipment works? Wouldn't they enjoy being able to fix minor problems by themselves?" In both cases, the answer is yes.

Management has long operated under the misconception that operators are unable to perform beyond the level of repetitive tasks. Meanwhile, operators yearn for greater responsibility. They are the ones who have the most intimate understanding of their equipment and its idiosyncrasies. In some cases, they are already performing minor maintenance but keep it a secret because they aren't supposed to do it.

A work group that is generally grossly overworked in manufacturing environments is engineers. In addition to overseeing maintenance of processes, they usually make all decisions about dispensation of any work that is even slightly out of the ordinary. Yet their expertise is needed more and more to develop improvements. How can they concentrate on improving processes if they are constantly troubleshooting and making minor decisions? So management looks at the large labor pool and asks, "Can we teach workers more abut the process of manufacturing? Will they be able to make sound decisions about material quality?" Again, the answer is yes.

Operators are the people closest to the work, so they can make sound decisions when unusual situations arise. Given enough good training, they can handle much of the routine engineering work. In my experience, line workers eagerly seek the opportunity to improve themselves. They want the chance to learn more about the place where they work, the jobs they perform, and the technical aspects of the processes they handle. In many industries, unions and management agree that without this change, a company cannot compete successfully. The ground is fertile for encouraging line workers to assume more responsibility for and ownership of their work.

The trend is underway. Many job descriptions now require more technical work. Many companies are trying new organizational designs to enhance this type of development. The current emphasis on teams vs. individual performers implies that team members will gradually learn to expand their skills repertoire to include elements currently defined as "outside their job." The ability to work well on a team and cooperate to enhance the quality and quantity of work produced will be emphasized in employment of the future.

The Japanese work force has become a phenomenon of intense interest to the U.S. business community and the country as a whole. Books, articles, and TV news segments depict the nature of that work force. A key trait is its dedication and commitment to the company's goals. People frequently attempt to explain away Japan's amazing level of commitment by arguing that the Japanese have a different culture and lifetime employment. However, in terms of our nation's ability to compete economically, the reasons for the difference are much less important than the *existence* of the difference.

The typical front-line Japanese worker knows a great deal about the company's business. The company continually presents information in meetings, posted on boards, and in documents. Workers discuss company business daily. They know who their major customers are. They know how customers feel about their product. They are challenged by meeting schedules. And they take the success or failure of their company personally. They feel intense involvement with the same information that management addresses. In addition, the best Japanese manufacturers provide their factory workers with real-time, on-line feedback on their team's performance. Quality monitors inform workers almost immediately of deviations from standard expectations. Problems are addressed shortly after they occur, preventing costly and lengthy reruns in production.

In contrast, in U.S. companies, management tends to emphasize performance numbers. Line workers receive occasional reports on performance. However, data about last week's or last month's quality performance does little to motivate or educate workers.

The fundamental principle of immediate feedback applies to business as well as education. If mistakes or process problems are identified as they happen, real learning and improvement can occur.

High-tech manufacturing, the newest and least-proven technology, has an inherent element of instability: instant response is required to keep manufacturing efforts on course. Manufacturing leading-edge products is like sailing a small boat: it requires watchfulness and sensitivity to minor changes. Manufacturing simple, low-tech products is more like operating a train on a set of tracks.

In fairness to American management, I think it has recognized the need for a more informed, motivated work force. Most companies distribute the company's performance information, including annual reports, to their employees. Many companies hold monthly or quarterly meetings to discuss business indicators. However, these carefully orchestrated management presentations miss a fairly large portion of the audiences to whom they could be useful.

Japanese workers have come to understand the meaning and implication of the business indicators they follow. Whether they learned the lingo in school or at the company, they understand what they hear. Most line workers in the U.S.A. do not understand the business reports they get. Month after month, year after year, management makes information presentations in good faith. And month after month, year after year, line workers snooze or "space out" at the meetings.

Management wants everyone to understand and be motivated by company goals. That is understandable. The missing link between desiring that goal and attaining it is the gap between two perspectives: workers see the world of the factory from one point of view, managers from another. To bridge that gap, training is needed. In this case, education might be appropriate—a program that takes workers step by step toward a basic literacy about the business and its key indicators. There could also be a companion program for managers that sensitizes them to the areas with which workers are having difficulty.

It is possible to bridge almost any gap between a reasonable, desired level of performance and the existing level. The key is to identify the desired state and the existing state. This is a basic principle of the training profession, and all effective trainers apply it in one way or another.

The evolution of the worker of the future must not be allowed to happen haphazardly. American industry must continually reevaluate to be certain it understands the requirements for the future worker. There must be a concerted, committed effort to provide the training needed to ensure the competitive edge of the American worker and American companies in the future.

3

State-of-the-Art Training

Excellence in training begins with a system suitable for its environment. Quality training cannot be described in terms of a particular technique. I have often encountered people who favored a particular training technique as the "correct" way to train. But prescribing a technique before one understands the overall operation and its requirements increases the risk of failure.

A personal example: while in the early stages of meeting with a client who was starting up a training program in the aerospace industry, I was told he wanted videotapes for the training. When I asked why, he said he had "heard from someone in the industry" that it was the way to go. I realized immediately he needed educating. Once we left the subject of videotapes and turned to *goals* of the training, our real work began. After a while he realized that selecting a training system customized to his needs would in turn determine the correct techniques. He eventually decided that the size of his business and its diversity of highly detailed jobs did not call for using video.

The concept of state-of-the-art training comes from upfront analysis of training opportunities. I cannot overemphasize the importance of this stage. Jumping into activity without sufficient data analysis can lead to misdirected actions and lost opportunities.

In management, the work of planning, educating, implementing, evaluating, and reporting are key areas. Thus, inadequate or inaccurate planning is the first potentially weak link in the chain or effort. Most managers consider themselves to be good planners. They take a project assignment and determine needed resources; they make realistic estimates of the time required for each step and come up with an achievable plan. Often they will complete the planning on schedule and be rewarded for it. Sounds feasible, right? That depends on what you really expect from yourself and/or the managers who work for you. In my scenario, the manager accepted an assignment and began planning. Taking instructions and responding is basically a *reactive* approach. To be *proactive,* a manager looks objectively at the assignment and asks such questions as, Does this project clearly contribute to the primary goals of the business plan? Is this the most effective activity to pursue at this time? What method of analysis was used to determine the potential improvement? How will the results be measured? Who are the customers, and will the results tie directly into their success?

Proactive managers clearly can make a much more significant contribution to planning. Looking ahead, they already would have studied the business plan to gain a sense of whether a project would require training. That kind of manager generally creates much more effective plans.

A comprehensive model of proactivity in training can be found in John Crosby's *Data Based Training* (1985). His approach addresses these issues directly and thoroughly. He focuses on high-tech manufacturing because of his extensive background in engineering, manufacturing management, and consulting in that area. What gives the book a particular richness is the fact that he did his doctoral work after spending many years in industry.

Crosby's primary thesis is that grounding in the business plan is an indispensable element in the management of training. That grounding, coupled with the ability to identify or develop key indicators and interpret their meanings accurately, significantly increases the effectiveness of training. Understanding the long-range goals and objectives of the company enables the training manager to think strategically and creatively about how training can contribute. It also gives managers the opportunity to integrate training for all the different functions of the organization and have meaningful conversations with other managers based on information gained from studying the business plan. A well-rounded training generalist is probably best suited to respond flexibly to changing needs in an organization.

For many people the idea of reading a business plan sounds about as appealing as filling out tax forms. That opinion arises from what Crosby calls the "myth" of the business plan. People imagine these plans are telephone-book-sized documents, written by lawyers, for no real reason other than to satisfy some obscure government requirement. In fact, a business plan is the product of some of the most detailed and soul-searching work of company management. In order to write a plan, top managers must take a thorough and objective look at their business from a number of viewpoints. For example, they must identify what distinguishes their company from similar ones, demonstrate a complete understanding of their industry as a whole, discuss sales and marketing strategies and their rationale, discuss production cost strategies, and much more. If you think of the business plan as the best work your top management can do, it becomes an adventure to study it. It may not provide pleasant, "armchair" reading, but it is well worth the effort.

Although the writing of a business plan is a common corporate activity, it is not a government requirement, and some companies may not have one. If your company doesn't, you can assemble much of the information on your own. (A section on how to do that appears in the appendix.)

What elements does a business plan typically contain?

1. Statement of your company and what distinguishes it from others in your field

Descriptions of

2. The industry of which your company is a part
3. Management team and organizational structure
4. Product/service provided by your company
5. Market segment served by your company
6. Total market place
7. Sales and marketing plan
8. Operations plan
9. Research and development (R&D) plan
10. Critical risks
11. Pro forma financials
12. Appendices.

(If you are unfamiliar with business plans, please review the list carefully. If this material is familiar to you, skim through the next section.)

1. *Statement of your company and what distinguishes it from other companies in your field.* This resembles an introduction to a speech or book. It gives the history of the company, how it was founded and by whom, and states the specific business of the company. It talks about who the major customers are and what they do with the company product. It allows top managers to put their best foot forward by explaining the particular specialties and strengths of their company as well as sharing their highest aspirations in the form of the company mission or charter.

2. *Information about the industry.* Under this heading, the reader learns about the industry of which the company is a part. A brief history of the industry and its customers sets the stage for a story about the industry leaders, how they achieved that status, and where this company fits into the picture. Past and current trends in the industry are highlighted, as are major changes or expected changes in such areas as technology and government regulation. Most people appreciate gaining this sort of perspective. It is useful not only in the effort to become a better planner, but it also provides some interesting background for stimulating lunchroom conversations.

3. *Management team and organizational structure.* This section has high human-interest value as well as planning implications. It discusses the background, education, and major accomplishments of the top management team. It lays out the collective philosophy of that team and assesses the team's strengths and weaknesses. It describes how the company is organized and what strategies are used in hiring and retaining key personnel, including compensation plans.

4. *Projects/services provided by your company.* An overall description is given of the company's products or services as well as a breakdown of major product families and how they relate to one another. An explanation and data are provided on the product life cycles, on how well-developed a product might be, and on how much longer it is expected to contribute to company profits. Also discussed in this section are special advantages such as competitive time advantages, patents, and proprietary processes.

5. *Market segment served by your company.* Here the customers are highlighted. You may discover some interesting details about the customer's products and how your product relates to them. Marketing, however, is the main theme, shown in crisp reports on the competition and how that knowledge strengthens the marketing plans. Critical selling issues—such as when a product has to be on the market to capture an opportunity—would be included here. The performance of major products in expanding or decreasing market share is reported and explained, as are plans to exploit new opportunities.

6. *Total market place.* This section presents a more global perspective, including the entire market "universe" of which your customers are a part. Trends and developments are explored, with comments on implications for the customer. Key indicators used by the larger industry segment are reported, with comments on how they are used in planning.

7. *Sales and marketing plan.* This item addresses the specifics of how the market research information was analyzed. If you have ever had the experience of trying to sell something

unusual, and mentioned your goal to anyone else, you have learned that everyone has an opinion of what people will buy and why. It can be enlightening to view the work of experts on a subject like this. Key customers and the plans to approach them, including advertising strategies, will also be found here. How marketing has anticipated problems and planned counter strategies is revealed. Pricing strategies and sales forecasts add the perspective of dollars and cents to this section.

8. *Operations plan.* Here you enter the world of a general manager, with data on manufacturing costs, plant capacities, key indicators, training, quality control, and automation, to name a few. Whether you know the world of manufacturing or not, this section can be exciting: in a sense, it's "where the action is." It evokes images of factories with lights burning around the clock, virtual hives of activity that hum and produce the goods that fuel our economy. The key indicators measure outputs, quality levels, inventory levels, services provided or, in some businesses, just billings. "Plant capacities" show the output potential of the facilities. Are they positioned with too much or too little capacity? How do they plan to produce the quality levels necessary to succeed in the market place?

9. *R&D plan.* What is the next generation of products being developed by your company? What does the future look like? How committed is the management to technological leadership? What percentage of sales are committed to research? This section can showcase some of the most creative and innovative people in your company.

10. *Critical risks.* When I previously discussed business plans and mentioned that the top management had to do some soul searching, this is one of the items to which I was referring. This section features a list of all of the major risks to the business and an analysis of each one. Included are plans for how to avoid or minimize losses in the event that any or all of these contingencies occurred. This section may cause feelings of insecurity, but it helps provide a more realistic outlook on the business.

11. *Pro forma financials.* This is a numbers section—forecasts of company earnings. The figures are broken down into major product categories. Cash flow items show anticipated expenses and income. Any assumptions behind these projections are stated up front.

12. *Appendices.* References and other supporting documents are attached here.

At this point you should look at your company's business plan, if you haven't already. Locating a copy may be as simple as asking your manager, who reaches into a drawer and hands it to you. You may have to be persistent if it's not readily available. If your company has a library, there may be a copy there, or other managers may have it. Finance and accounting managers can often help. Keep in mind that your request may seem unusual, since people don't pop into managers' offices asking for a business plan everyday. If asked to explain your request, do not get defensive, but simply explain the exercise you are undertaking.

Once you have assembled these data, you can integrate them with other information you have been absorbing from your environment. I find it helpful to play with the information, creating graphs and charts that reorganize the data in unusual ways, which can lead to startling discoveries. From the analysis, you can determine the "high leverage points" for training intervention. *High leverage points* are areas in which an organization will receive the most benefit in terms of return on dollars spent. Strategic decisions are the only overriding factors. It may be in the company's best interest to place training emphasis on preparing for the future. This will become obvious from analysis of the business plan and discussion with top management.

Only after determining leverage points should you attempt a detailed analysis of what is required for the training that will address those areas. For example, suppose a telecommunications company has identified from the data that its repair technicians are returning to rework repairs 35 percent of the time. The average time for a repair is 3.5 hours. Once these data are summarized as a monthly or yearly cost, the company begins to understand what opportunities exist. The company factors in 100 technicians with an average annual salary and benefit cost of $40,000. That equals $4,000,000. If 35 percent of their time is being spent in reworking repairs instead of getting it right the first time, the company loses (wastes) $1,400,000. This information should be explored to determine areas for training.

Another area to consider would be the 3.5-hour average repair time. One could study the technicians to learn whether there is a significant time difference between expert performance and the average. For example, if the best technicians average 1.0 hours on repairs, it is possible that training could reduce the average time of the rest. This would yield the equivalent of extra head count at no additional cost after training.

Once the problems are understood and the skills deficiencies identified, the task of designing the training programs begins. At this point, technique comes into play. Choice of technique depends on the kind of training to be done.

This chapter has explained how to begin plans for state-of-the-art training, which ensures that department activities make maximum contribution to the company. When you deliver high-quality, focused training, you have achieved state of the art. When you continually analyze and process new information about the company as a business to make proactive decisions, you have achieved state of the art.

4

Technician Training

A key strategy at many companies is to use automation and robotics ever increasingly. Their rationale is that robots consistently produce a quality of work that exceeds human capability, and automation provides a computer-controlled work flow that maximizes factory output. Both can work for great lengths of time without pause. They are expected to produce higher and more reliable quality products at a lower manufacturing cost.

The motivation to decrease reliance on human labor results mainly from competition. Consumers naturally select the product that gives the best value for the dollar and rarely care about the product's manufacture or origin. Selections in the market place tend to be based on quality, reliability, and price.

In some industries, the cost of opening a factory has increased tenfold in less than two decades. This is largely because the cost of sophisticated equipment has skyrocketed. For example, in the semiconductor industry the intensity of capital is so high that price tags of $500,000 for one piece of equipment are not unusual. The manufacture of microprocessors requires hundreds of pieces of equipment, many commanding high prices. The current rate of inflation for semiconductor equipment is estimated at 22-28 percent. That means equipment tends to depreciate 66 percent in 3-5 years!

Automation is not common in most high-tech manufacturing, although it is widely used in the product design phase with the application of computer-aided design (CAD). What *is* the norm, however, is ever more sophisticated equipment and long-range plans to phase in automation. As the cost of equipment soars, it becomes more essential to maximize the output of each piece. In industry terms, the word is *uptime,* or how long the equipment stays up and running. In *downtime,* the equipment stands idle. The ability of a factory to keep equipment running according to plan is critical. Some factories have backup equipment for emergencies. But some equipment is just too expensive or specialized for a backup. In the latter case, production comes to a stop when the equipment is down.

Unexpected downtime tends to be costly in a high-tech factory. People may be idle and products ruined if the manufacturing process is time sensitive and schedules are missed. Because equipment of any kind needs maintenance, that activity must be planned. For example, your car should have an oil change every so many thousand miles; if you neglect to do it, you will eventually have significant downtime on your engine. High-tech equipment runs under the same principle, but maintenance intervals are much shorter: some equipment requires minor maintenance every eight hours and major maintenance weekly. In the aviation field, minor maintenance occurs after every flight.

The maintenance of equipment today requires sophisticated skills and knowledge. Technicians who keep the equipment running need knowledge in such areas as electronics, vacuum technology, and mechanics in addition to enough familiarity with the manufacturing or operating systems in order to troubleshoot. (Soon, fiber optics and optoelectronics will be common skill requirements.) Such technicians constitute the leading edge of their industries and are a critical factor in their industries' manufacturing capability. When new models of equipment are introduced into a manufacturing environment, they cannot be considered reliable unless trained technicians are available to keep them functioning.

Technical skills can be so critical and so specialized that equipment vendors frequently give classes on their own equipment and charge between $500 and $2,000 per student for a week's training. Classes are generally given at the equipment vendor's own location, which can involve travel expenses. It is not uncommon for technicians to attend 1-2 courses a year. For technicians in the armed forces and high-tech industries, expenditures for training can amount to over 10 percent of their annual salaries.

Aside from equipment, many high-tech manufacturing processes require specialized environments and materials, such as ultra-clean air and ultra-pure chemicals and gases. The maintenance of pure air systems in cleanrooms is a specialty in itself. Maintaining a water system with specific electrical and biological properties requires high levels of expertise. Extensive training and experience are required to run equipment and maintain an environment for such sophisticated systems.

Skilled technicians are in short supply today. Recruiters must search wider and wider geographical areas in order to find them. (Recall that the U.S. Bureau of Labor has projected a 330-percent increase in all types of maintenance technicians between 1985 and 2000.) Many different kinds of specialized equipment require many different kinds of specialists, making it difficult to locate someone with the precise experience and expertise needed. For this reason, companies willingly pay a premium to lure an expert from a competitor. They will also offer generous incentives to induce a technician to relocate.

Hiring an expert for an immediate need solves a problem temporarily. However, as soon as a new kind of equipment arrives, a recruiter is back in the same fix. It is not feasible to keep hiring experts every time new skills or equipment are needed.

Most equipment vendors advertise some kind of training support for their system. The extent of that support among various vendors ranges from excellent to nonexistent. Often, company field service representatives work with technicians to help them keep things running. The most sound approach to bringing in new equipment involves ensuring that you have a repeatable, detailed training program to accompany it. In the last few years, many firms have included technical training content objectives in their purchase orders for new equipment. They have made portions of payment contingent on the original equipment manufacturer delivering that training and ensuring a measurable attainment of objectives by inhouse technicians. If the vendor cannot supply what you need, you may have to build courses inhouse or contract it out with independent training developers.

Something worthy of note about original equipment manufacturers (OEMs) and the training and support of the equipment they sell: Figure 1 shows that during the first six months a piece of equipment is on the factory floor, its uptime is quite high. During this time period, the machine is being started up and bugs are being worked out. It is also the manufacturer's warranty period, so the OEM has field service people working closely with the factory on installation.

During the warranty period, the field service representatives have a high degree of control over how the equipment is serviced, and the OEM gathers data about the machine's characteristics and failures in the field.

After the warranty has elapsed, many factories begin to make proprietary modifications on the equipment. They do not want the competition to know their tricks, so they limit access to the equipment to company personnel. Field service representatives still answer calls for help with problems. But reduced exposure to equipment and machine performance data in the field leaves OEMs short on information. Vendors need more information about how a product performs throughout its entire operational life in order to improve the product and training to operate it.

Therefore, industry in this country would be enhanced if companies negotiated confidentiality agreements with their vendors (OEMs) and then supported them with access to the equipment and machine performance data. OEMs could then redesign equipment based on a true analysis of how it performs in the field and how it is used by customers. In addition, vendors could provide better training to handle the failures that will occur throughout a machine's lifetime.

Sale and use of high-tech equipment resemble those of high-performance vehicles. Each system, each unique piece of equipment, has its own signature of performance strength and weakness. The generic training from an equipment vendor usually won't be enough to sustain the system at the level the company buyer needs. There is often a technical interface gap. From the OEM's viewpoint, the product is working according to specifications. From the company's viewpoint, the product may not fit the requirements of the production line. Therefore, detailed training objectives formalized in the purchase agreement can help alleviate frustration and disappointment for both parties. Vendor training can be a tremendous asset, but a company may still need a program of support for that system in the company *setting*.

Some OEM vendors take their training responsibilities seriously. Others do not. In all fairness, however, original equipment manufacturers must dedicate most of their resources to manufacturing or upgrading their equipment models. Some of them have staffs too small to allow them to offer a serious training program.

Equipment manufacturers buy 80 percent of the components for their machines. They may not be experts on why or how a component works. They develop their systems by interfacing components purchased from a variety of sources, thereby creating a uniquely proprietary piece of equipment. Consequently, even with the best of intentions, an equipment manufacturer may not be able to explain every last detail of the machinery it manufactures.

In every factory, technicians must be very familiar with the equipment, old and new. How they receive training depends on company management. There may be an inhouse training resource dedicated to providing the training. The company may rely on the equipment vendor's training inhouse

Figure 1. *Equipment Downtime/Uptime*

Courtesy of Integrated Semiconductor Training, Inc.

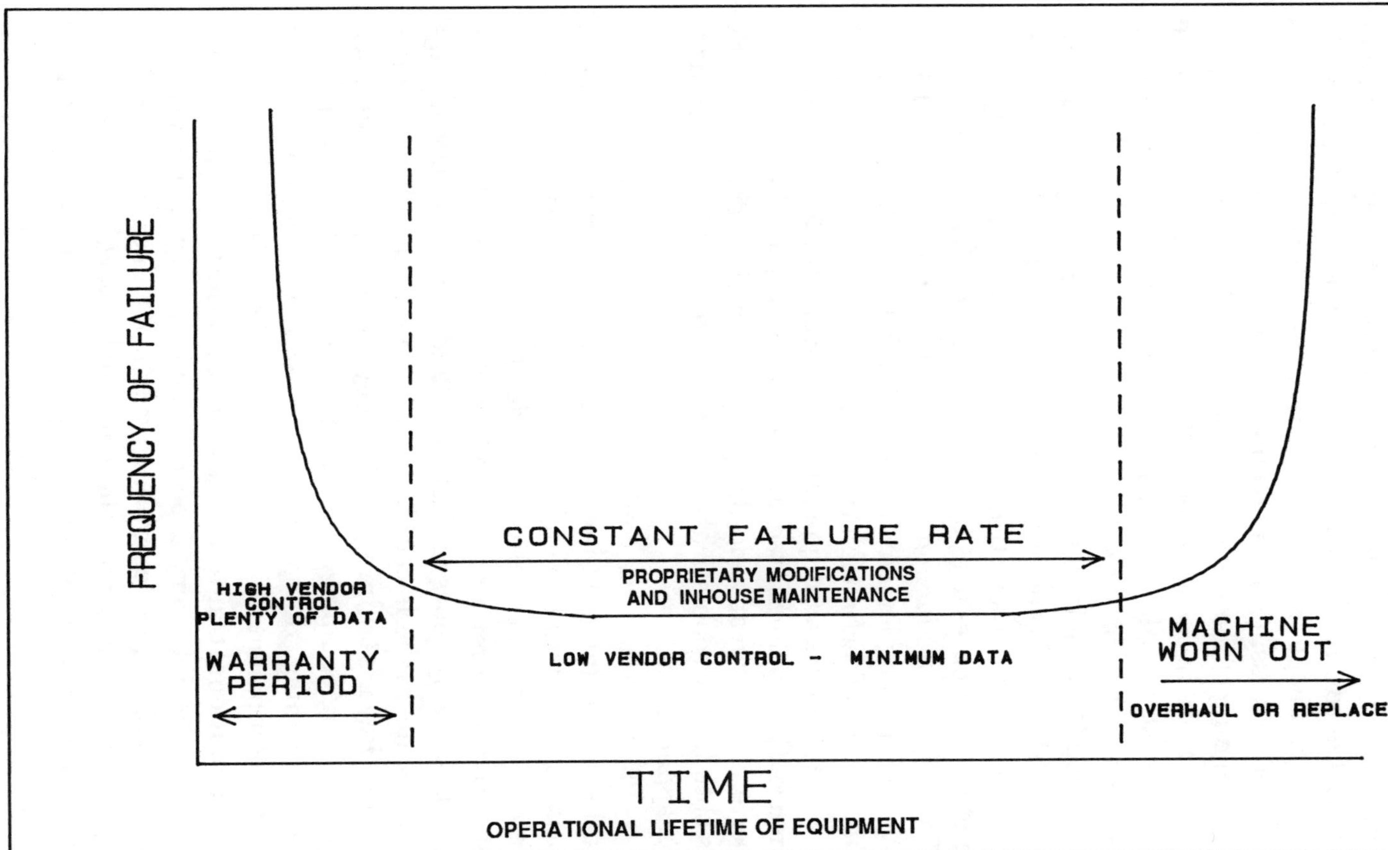
FREQUENCY OF FAILURE
HIGH VENDOR CONTROL
PLENTY OF DATA
WARRANTY PERIOD
CONSTANT FAILURE RATE
PROPRIETARY MODIFICATIONS AND INHOUSE MAINTENANCE
LOW VENDOR CONTROL - MINIMUM DATA
MACHINE WORN OUT
OVERHAUL OR REPLACE
TIME
OPERATIONAL LIFETIME OF EQUIPMENT

or outside. It may use private training facilities specializing in what it needs. It may ask technicians to teach one another. Or it may just hope that people get trained by osmosis.

Often missing in the training effort is a fundamental understanding of the skills a technician really needs and the best way to train in those skills. Following is a description of some of the best work I have seen on the actual science of training equipment technicians.

Dolf Payer, founder of Skills Training Systems in Cupertino, California, is one of the most experienced trainers in Silicon Valley's microelectronics industry. He has recently completed an impressive body of work entitled *Maintenance Training for Reduction of Unscheduled Down-Time* (1986). Written to complement his consulting, the book explains the fine details of technician training.

Payer offers a unique combination of knowledge and experience. He supplemented two decades of technical training experience with an advanced degree in cognition. Thus, his work is both highly sophisticated and attuned to real-world, hands-on applications.

Payer's approach centers around inhouse training. His technical training philosophy departs from the traditional models: it is data driven, with an easy statistical model that relies only on practicality for its design. He cautions, "Beware of activity training programs." In other words, if a recruiter wants so many hours of electronics and so many hours of diagnostics, he or she is counting hours, not focusing on training *results*. Payer's training has two key goals: improved methods of repairing equipment and cost savings. In Payer's maintenance training, the goal is a measurable increase in uptime and, if equipment fails, a decrease in repair time.

Traditional training tries to instruct the technician generally—i.e., about every aspect of the equipment. It covers all known types of problems and gives the technician a lot of theory about how and why the equipment works. The delivery method tends to be predominantly classroom style, with participants seated, viewing numerous diagrams and schematics and listening to a lecture. The training usually occurs in one- or two-week blocks.

Payer advocates designing technician training by ranking downtime faults based on the most frequent and costly problems. In his model, detailed analysis of equipment downtime yields information leading to what he calls a "First-Fault Module." Usually a single fault occurs 30 percent of the time.

Payer gives much emphasis to the gathering and sorting of the data used to determine these decisions. He divides the data into two major categories: quantitative and environmental. Quantitative data include such items as mean downtimes, skill levels of technicians, cost of repair by types, potentials for improvement, and review criteria. Environmental factors include the human components of the job. A data-gathering method called "major concerns" taps into each person as an internal consultant to the firm by discovering his or her perspectives from a hands-on and subconscious viewpoint. It addresses mental blocks to change and what is required to remove them. It discovers what is and isn't working from the technician's viewpoint. Payer develops the major concerns data into a prescription-model-path for training and organizational purposes.

Accurate and detailed data gathering characterizes Payer's model. Training methods will depend on what phase of training you are conducting. If you are in the initial stage of targeting the problems training will address, you will find production reports and cost accounting data indispensable. If you are trying to identify content experts, you will want to correlate top performance scores with reputation.

Analyzing expertise is a much more intimate process. Actually video- and audiotaping the troubleshooting as it is being done is considered the most desirable method. This enables the designer to review the tapes with the expert and probe for subtleties. Payer offers an analysis method for creating troubleshooting maps that yields valuable training material.

If you are in the design phase of training, you can apply design rules that utilize cognitive principles to determine the best approach.

Collecting extensive data will help you ensure that you are targeting the precise kind of training needed. (Most companies fail to take advantage of the benefits of data collection.) A targeted approach enables companies to train technicians on a *need-to-know,* rather than a *nice-to-know,* basis. Technical training is complex enough without the added confusion of extraneous material.

Using a modular-exercise design of training to correct a specific problem until it is mastered is effective because it is focused. After a technician has had enough time to take a number of service calls on the primary defect and become familiar with it, a class on the second most important defect is taken. The training follows a statistical Pareto rule: 80 percent of the downtime results from 20 percent of the service calls. The rest of the calls are for "rare" defects and are addressed in training only after the critical 20 percent of machine calls have been mastered. The modular exercise trains technicians in how to search, detect faults, troubleshoot, make prescriptions, do repairs, and evaluate repairs in a way resembling that of the experts. It trains by use of carefully introduced blocks of information with immediate application.

"Rare" defects are generally taught by simulation rather than on the actual equipment because of difficulties arising from unusual problems that can occur during training. The training department continually collects parts that have failed because of unusual causes. The training department asks to be informed when a rare defect occurs so that the troubleshooting can be captured for later use. Although emphasis is on completing the critical 20 percent of defects, the job isn't complete until the handling of rare defects has been taught. This is especially important when technicians move from regular day shift to an off shift. They must be knowledgeable about rare defects because less help is available.

Because technical positions are active and equipment oriented, technical training must take that into account. Between 60 and 90 percent of the training should be conducted hands on. A guiding principle is that technicians get out of their chairs 8-15 times a day; therefore, matching an action-oriented training style to their normal work style is more likely to hold their attention.

The principle of "positive transfer" also supports the hands-on approach. The more closely training matches real-life working conditions, the more likely that skills learned will be applied on the job. For example, 100 percent transfer occurs when the training is done on line, with the actual piece of equipment, solving real troubleshooting problems. Zero transfer occurs when the training and/or exercises don't match on-line technical demands. Negative transfer occurs when the trainee receives incorrect data and is taught inappropriate habits: mistakes must be unlearned.

In order to retain the benefits of training, a technician must work regularly on the equipment, beginning right after training. If this immediate application occurs, trainees will forget less than 20 percent of what they learned. However, if there is a week's delay, the information loss will probably be about 40 percent. If there is a delay greater than two weeks, most of the benefits of the training will be lost.

To enhance the benefits, a company should provide positive feedback. Technicians generally receive either negative feedback or none. Managers should include in maintenance training some form of feedback that recognizes accomplishment. Giving out certificates is not enough. Most technicians would be more satisfied if they could show their manager, *at the machine,* how they found an actual problem and fixed it. This approach not only reinforces the learning but improves morale and reduces employee turnover.

Another interesting and creative response to bridging the gap between training needs and vendor offerings is the evolution of *independent providers* of training on popular industrial equipment. These providers tend to be technical experts on the equipment and, in the best cases, in instructional design as well.

Integrated Semiconductor Training, Inc. (IST), a firm based in Tempe, Arizona, represents what I consider a prototype of technical training firms of the future. It is staffed by people highly experienced in microelectronics. The staff offers expertise in management, equipment, industrial psychology, instructional design, and statistics—a multitalented group, indeed.

The firm utilizes data-based training methodologies to develop its business plans. For example, it obtained data on equipment downtime from its potential customers and identified training needs industry-wide. The equipment training program took off and now boasts a customer list that includes Rockwell International, Digital Equipment Corporation, Fairchild Industries, Hughes, AMCC, Intel, and Northern Telecom. The firm has identified other areas of need in industry in the same fashion and has developed programs for them. Statistical quality control is one area in which it has excelled.

Technician training is a major portion of IST's business. The philosophy and approach to the training are refreshingly functional. Through analysis of reasons for equipment downtime in factories, the company made two major discoveries. One was that equipment was often shut down for reasons that were not technically sound. In other words, equipment labeled as "down" was actually still able to run correctly. This problem was one of communication among technicians, operators, engineers, and managers using different vocabularies and misunderstanding one another's criteria.

The second major problem was the impractical approach technicians took to repairing equipment. Technicians were keeping equipment down while they puzzled over minute, component-level solutions, when they should merely have replaced the subassembly and turned the equipment back to production.

IST technician training takes the systems approach. It recognizes that the number of components in equipment is so high today it is impractical to try to teach a technician every detail. Instead, the focus should be on the total interaction of the equipment's modules or subassemblies. The major goal is to give a technician a thorough understanding of the system as an operating unit, with a function to perform in a factory.

It is essential that the technician also understand the contribution a piece of equipment makes to the total process of manufacturing a product. Therefore, the technician needs to know about *processes* at the plant. Only with this knowledge can a good judgment be made about whether a piece of equipment is ready to support the process.

IST requires technicians to learn how equipment works from the user's end. If technicians cannot perform an operator's job and run the equipment without assistance, they cannot be effective in understanding repair requests. (An analogy would be a car mechanic who has never learned how to drive.)

Finally, technicians are taught to make *economic* rather than technical decisions. Once they have learned the basic economics of a factory and understand the impact and cost of downtime, they can make better decisions. A piece of production equipment can cost the factory $10,000 for each hour it is not available to run the product. Therefore, it is critical that the technician think in terms of how quickly the equipment can be returned to production and not become seduced into wasting valuable uptime hours searching for a faulty transistor.

The technician is trained to isolate the smallest module or subassembly that must be replaced in order to get the equipment back into production. The module or subassembly can be repaired off line on a work bench in the lab. The economies of scale make decisions easier: should a technician spend five hours solving problems with one component to avoid replacing a $300 subassembly when it costs the factory $50,000 to have the machine out of service? Of course not. But until the technician understands the basics of the system, the choices are not that clear.

Upon successful completion of this kind of course, a technician can repair equipment using the systems approach, operate the equipment, communicate effectively with coworkers, make decisions based on economics, and bring equipment up from a dead stop to return it to production—goals on every equipment manager's wish list.

A tribute to IST's equipment training program is the enthusiasm from participating technicians. They have given outstanding scores to the evaluators, indicating they felt the material to be of high quality and on target for the real world. Technicians are exposed to so much training in their careers that their opinion of a class is a good gauge of its quality. Another tribute is the uptime improvements reported by customers.

IST also operates a centralized microelectronics training facility in San Diego. The $2-million facility contains a simulated wafer fabrication and assembly area and is a joint partnership between microelectronics companies in the area and the Private Industry Countil, which administers JTPA funds. The Microelectronics Training Center trains disadvantaged workers and has achieved exemplary performance ratings for providing employers with skilled operators.

The center now teaches cleanroom procedures, wire bonding, die attaching, surface mounting, and soldering. It is working with its customers—microelectronics companies in the area—to develop a centralized training service for supervisory and technician training as well.

By now, the role of technicians in the factory of the future should be clear. Because of the influence they have on the costs of running the business, they will be a company's make-or-break factor. Therefore, the importance of their training cannot be overemphasized.

5

What Can We Learn from Japanese Training Methods?

The manufacturing excellence of the Japanese spurs their ability to penetrate valuable world markets. They increase their market share in industries they target almost at will. They can manage this because they continually set the world standards on quality and price. They accomplish this feat through long-term strategies for market penetration, product development, and manpower development.

The overall philosophy of Japanese industry is based on a military model and operates under the belief that success in the market place resembles victory on the battlefield: there is a victor and a vanquished. As in warfare, there must be relentless dedication to strategic planning in order to beat competitors. This principle applies not only to marketing and product development but also to human resource development.

The approach the Japanese take to training reveals their human resourcce strategy. As in so many other aspects of their work, training is planned and executed in a diligent and disciplined manner.

The level at which training is planned and reviewed in major Japanese firms indicates the importance they give it. Most major Japanese electronics firms have a senior-vice-president level of position responsible for training. CEOs review training issues monthly and/or quarterly.

A high degree of commitment to training appears at every level in Japanese manufacturing organizations. At the factory level, for example, general managers review training monthly and formally recognize individual training accomplishments.

Managers at all levels are held strictly accountable for the execution of employee training plans, which include technical and nontechnical skills development.

In the case of technical skills development, employees are expected to spend most of their time practicing the skill they have just been taught. The supervisor is expected to ensure they are not diverted from this portion of their training. Sending a student to technical school and not supporting on-the-job follow-up is considered a serious failure in a manager.

Human resource management is a supervisor's primary responsibility. Employee performance is not measured by output because that is a team accomplishment. Supervisors train, develop, and enforce policy and guide employees in their development. Negative attitudes toward training will damage a career, so the follow-through rate on training is high.

The companies have high standards for their employees. Extensive testing is done, beginning at the time of employment application and continuing throughout an employee's career. For example, there is selection testing to ensure that people who are hired are offered jobs most suitable for their success. Upon completion of any training, the employee must pass a test. The employee is expected to demonstrate proficiency according to specified criteria. Should these criteria not be met, the employee wil be given further training.

In addition to rigorous company standards, there are national certification requirements for many technical jobs. Operators, technicians, and engineers may be required to pass national certification tests.

Skills competitions are held, much like sporting events. Teams and individual experts from the same industries compete in elimination trials. For example, there might be a competition in assembling cameras. First the factory holds a competition; then that champion competes with other factory champions until there is a company winner; then there is national competition for companies in that business. They go so far as to seek competition with other countries, where possible, to establish a world champion.

In terms of manpower planning, Japanese firms have some straightforward ideas. They want to have the right people in the right places at the right times. This is not something they leave to chance. The companies have ten-year plans, and they develop products and people to match those plans. It is not unusual for an employee to have a ten-year training plan in place shortly after joining a company.

In hiring, Japanese companies look carefully at personality as well as skills. They like to hire people who have a balance of good skills, good personal habits, good health, and high motivation. Companies accept employees from college, high school, or junior high school. They believe a young person with high aptitude is an excellent investment, and they may develop a training plan for that person that is essentially lifelong. A student who is lucky enough could join a company while still in junior high school and become a certified engineer within fifteen years.

Companies always schedule indoctrination for new employees. The basic orientation lasts three days to three weeks for nonmanagement positions. This introduction is devoted to building loyalty to the company, extensive education about the company's history, and reinforcing work ethics. Skills training may begin during this time as well. For management, the basic training period runs two months to two years and includes extensive exposure to all aspects of the company's business. This exposure is usually accomplished through job rotations.

The Japanese tend to analyze issues carefully before reaching a conclusion. However, once they reach a conclusion and study its meaning, they move decisively into action. This is apparently why they have invested so heavily in training ($70-100 million annually for each of the top electronics firms). One could point out that the scale of those firms is generally larger than that of their U.S counterparts. However, direct comparison can be made by looking at annual dollars invested per employee: for training, Japanese firms outspend American companies about 4-5 times. They know this strategy has brought them to their commanding position in industry today and will keep them ahead of the competition tomorrow.

Large, corporate educational institutions provide university-level curricula in a variety of subjects. An employee can obtain education—from a high school diploma to an advanced degree in systems engineering—from the company school. Corporate institutions support rotational job programs for manager training. They also provide generic courses at the individual sites.

Factories all have their own training departments as well, to develop and deliver training specific to the site. It is not unusual for the larger factories to have a training facility that replicates actual production lines—a "training factory," if you will.

The following timeline is typical of a management training plan in Japanese electronic firms:

Orientation—1 month

Visits to company factories—1 month

Manufacturing training—3 months

Advanced training—20 months (in classroom and on the job)

Written thesis presented to senior management panel.

A machine technician's training might take the following schedule:

First major piece of equipment training—1,500 hours (including lecture, school, and on-the-job practice)

Advanced training—2,500 hours (over several years, cross training on other machines, automation training, electronics, mechanics, robotics, software)

Demonstration of ability to assemble and operate a robot

Achievement of certification.

An example of the fine performance such training buys: the average reported equipment uptime in the top Japanese semiconductor factories is approximately 96 percent. Compare that with the reported 53 percent average in the U.S.A.

Although the methods of training at different companies vary considerably, Japan's commitment to training is clearly serious.

What can Americans learn from all this? The most important lesson lies more in overall philosophy than in technique. . . .

The educational technology community in the United States is outstanding. If there were a way to compare our capabilities in instructional design or simulation technology with Japan's, I think we would be the hands-down winner. Our professional training community is good.

But where we fail is at the senior-management level, in the planning and execution of long-range strategies—in which Japan excels. Its system is not incredibly creative or sophisticated: it simply works through commitment, dedication, and follow-through from all levels of management. The Japanese make a formal commitment to an employee's career. They take each employee's career seriously and work with that person to help him or her achieve success. What is good for the company is good for the employee, and vice versa, and the system is planned with that in mind.

The Japanese understand the principle of forbearance. They demonstrate self-discipline on a national scale. They humbly do the groundwork, patiently build their infrastructures, and emerge as a formidable opponent. They plan carefully, make decisions, and follow through.

This is a key lesson for us. If we determine that training is an area we must build up for strategic reasons, then we must commit for the duration. Serious efforts will be required to educate people about a company's commitment to training. This may be the frontier where our corporate cultures can get a toehold on the self-discipline needed to regain our industrial power.

We must also make the transition from considering an employee's career as incidental to the company's goals, to considering it *part* of the company's goals. Granted, we have a far more transient work force than that of Japan; however, trust and commitment must begin somewhere. And it is well-known that the "choice" companies in the U.S.A. have low turnover rates.

It should be evident how essential training is to our nation's survival and resurgence as the world's leader in industry. However, we should not resort to knee-jerk reactions. Japan's success in training has resulted from careful analysis, planning, and long-term commitment. Hence, careful analysis, establishing long-term training strategies, and sticking with them, or intelligently modifying them, is our proper response.

6

Critical-Industries Training: When Practice Must Produce Perfection

After many years of working with training professionals, I have observed what happens when they lack adequate recognition and funding. They tend to lose scope and vigor in their ideas for training programs and strategies. Companies that neglect their technical training efforts tend to institutionalize low energy and lack of innovation, not only in their trainers but their line workers as well. Line trainers can have enormous impact on the morale of the rest of the workers. So much can be accomplished with training when there is a sincere and enlightened commitment behind it.

The technical training strategies of most U.S. industries tend to be unimaginative, partly because trainers don't feel *empowered* to be creative. By looking at the methodologies and techniques of what I call "critical-industry training," we can expand the horizons of people not involved in that type of work. *Critical industries* are those whose work, by its nature, has extremely dire consequences if failure occurs.

Although we all agree that high-quality work is the first principle of successful manufacturing, not every industry absolutely requires it.

In the critical industries, however, flawless performance is required—usually, for reasons of safety. For example, a commercial airline pilot must be thorough: almost-perfect performance can lead to a crash. Similarly, in the operation of nuclear power plants, the public expects perfect performance and is rightfully intolerant of failure. When human lives are at stake, cost justifications diminish in importance. The philosophy is, We must do whatever it takes—there is no margin for error.

Nuclear power plant training is certainly an area in which we expect all operations to be done correctly. This training falls roughly into two user categories: the military and the utilities. Although both basically have the goal of perfect performance, the conditions under which they operate differ.

To the military, power plants are engines that drive surface ships and submarines. They are, in every sense, high-performance nuclear reactors. They must function, when necessary, under relatively adverse environmental conditions. Ship reactors are, of course, much smaller than the shore-based utility power generators.

The utilities, on the other hand, are in the business of generating and selling electricity. For their purposes, large reactors are cost effective. They may operate two or even three reactors at the same site in order to maximize the efficiency of support services, such as personnel and transmission. The utilities are heavily regulated by the Nuclear Regulatory Commission (NRC) and cannot operate without an NRC license.

In the United States, a significant portion of the population has always felt threatened by the presence of nuclear power plants. These people have been dismayed by the results of the disaster in Chernobyl. Interestingly enough, in France, the nuclear power industry is accepted by the vast majority of the population. In France and in the United States, training is considered a vital element in ensuring the safe and efficient operation of nuclear plants. Both countries have excellent training programs, and both certify operators. The evolution of the industry's training efforts will provide an interesting perspective on critical-industry training.

In the mid 1960s, federal regulations were established for the nuclear power industry. They imposed some rudimentary training requirements the utilities found they were not capable of meeting. Although they were staffed with bright, technologically competent engineers and technicians, they were unable to develop the detailed and sophisticated training required. It was not simply a matter of establishing training to meet the stringent federal requirements. Because the utility industry had not previously developed any widespread *need* for training, it did not have the *resources* to address the requirements.

Some utilities attempted to utilize the university systems for training. This effort was largely unsuccessful because universities are, by design, educational institutions, not training institutions. Also, nuclear power technology was too new for any university system to have established any reasonable base of information and reference.

Therefore, private consultants offering training services got most of the business. The consultants were engineers with a lot of experience in the industry. Some were better than others at the task.

In order to grasp the magnitude of a nuclear power plant operator's job, picture yourself in the control room—a thousand-square-foot room filled with computers, switches, dials, digital readouts lights, and other equipment; in the center, a couple of desks and a control board run by two or three people. The critical work of controlling power levels is done here. Only a federally licensed operator can handle the power controls. This person's knowledge and judgment are relied upon to keep the plant operating safely and, in particular, to respond appropriately to abnormal situations.

The federal regulations were implemented in 1965, but any sense of comfort or security with the safety of nuclear power facilities vanished in March of 1979, when the reactor core of unit No. 2 melted down at the Three Mile Island plant in Pennsylvania. Thousands of people were evacuated from their homes, in some cases never to return.

The government sponsored several in-depth studies of that accident in order to determine the root causes, both in terms of hardware failure and personnel errors. The "Rogovin report" (U.S. Nuclear Regulatory Commission, 1980) listed as a primary cause "inadequate training of licensed operators." It revealed there had been very little hands-on or "real-time" practice in the training.

The government then moved to create exact prescriptions for the training of plant operators. However, the utilities appealed to the government for an opportunity to regulate themselves as an industry. The government agreed to allow the industry to make a proposal, resulting in assignment of the task to the Institute of Nuclear Power Operations (INPO).

INPO is an industry organization established to promote professionalism and exchange of information on industry problems. All U.S. nuclear utilities are members of INPO. NRC agreed to allow INPO to establish guidelines and accredit training programs in the industry. INPO accredits the training of both licensed and nonlicensed nuclear power plant personnel. INPO-accredited training programs use the Systems Approach to Training (SAT), patterned after military training techniques based on Instructional Systems Development (ISD).

Because the training had to be hands on and real time in nature, the utilities had only two alternatives. One was to use the actual control rooms of operating facilities for training, which would entail taking the plants off line at some point to give the trainees full access to the controls. The other alternative was to build teaching reactors that exactly simulated the real ones. Although teaching reactors are an enormously expensive proposition, taking a plant off line and shutting down reactors would be far more costly.

Most commercial reactors in the United States that are in operation, or almost in operation, have a control room simulator identical to the actual control room. However, NRC will accept training on another plant's simulator if the differences are small and not of great consequence to accident diagnosis and response. Because the configuration of each power plant is somewhat different, its control room and simulator form a unique set. The NRC is extremely strict in its licensing and is planning increased emphasis on the operator's ability to demonstrate proficiency on the simulator for both normal and abnormal occurrences.

The simulator is a fully functioning facility that runs programs that can last several days. This capability allows operators to get a feel for how the system operates over time periods that parallel those of the real job. This condition is necessary because the decisions that operators make on the job are based not only on immediate data but on analysis of trends. In addition to acquiring the necessary skills to operate and shut down a plant, an operator has a crucial role to play in the event of an accident.

On April 26, 1986, the Soviet-built reactor in Chernobyl was undergoing a safety test. The reactor operators violated six key safety procedures, ultimately causing explosions that released large quantities of radioactive materials into the air. (The event is remembered as the worst accident in nuclear power history.) Soviet power plants are built without containment structures, which are required under U.S. standards. The importance of the containment buildings in protecting people and the environment is critical.

Until the disaster, U.S. operator training in simulators included emergency response training only for Day One of an accident. Now, larger and more complex computers are being added to simulators to allow practice of loss-control procedures for a week or more after an accident.

NRC licenses operators and audits the training. It is also conducting a comprehensive internal training effort in order to be more effective in its audits. It must use simulators to train its own people as well. Until recently, it leased time on commercial simulators. NRC has now purchased a simulator of its own in order to improve training and to be a credible agency to the industry. (It now has a Westinghouse pressurized water reactor simulator.)

Two years of training are required for licensing as a reactor operator. However, before applicants can be accepted for training, they must have a significant amount of time in the industry, usually as technicians in a plant. A utility will invest $250,000-$400,000 in training an operator. To become a senior reactor operator requires still more training and involves additional expense for the utility. (See figure 2.)

A typical operator training program will include 16-20 weeks of academic training followed by two weeks of classes in the plant. The in-plant class is followed by hands-on work with the simulator or under close supervision in the real control room. As skills are acquired, qualification cards are signed by the trainer, verifying performance of the required exercises. This alternation of classroom or self-paced training with hands-on practice makes up the two years of training. The hands-on practice is supervised by experienced operator/trainers who are very conscientious with the trainees. Training for the operator's federal licensing continues for another sixteen months.

All workers at a nuclear facility receive extensive training in their jobs. This meticulous approach to training is driven by safety-motivated regulations. In addition to the training, government requirements address equipment maintenance. An interesting byproduct of the safety considerations has been the performance of nuclear plants in comparison with that of conventional fossil fuel plants. The preventive maintenance programs, coupled with careful training, have yielded significantly higher facility availabilities. The efficiency of the nuclear plants exceeds that of fossil fuel plants as well.

Government regulations for fossil plants are nowhere near as stringent as for nuclear plants. There are no preventive maintenance schedules that must be followed. Instrument calibration is not inspected by the government, and licensing is not required. However, fossil plant managers impressed by the performance of the nuclear plants, are starting to emulate many of their procedures, including training and careful preventive maintenance programs.

How has the U.S. Navy handled nuclear power?

The evolution of the nuclear Navy provides another interesting insight into the application of training in the nuclear field. Admiral Hyman G. Rickover was a true visionary. His dream of a nuclear Navy has become a reality, and it appears he was able to build it largely by demonstrating the success and safety record of his ships.

Westinghouse developed the original Navy reactor plants at the same time the civilian utility plants were established. It was clear from the beginning that ship-based reactors could not be surrounded with the huge containment structures of shore-based reactors.

Admiral Rickover convinced the Atomic Energy Commission (forerunner to the NRC) that having highly qualified and highly trained operators would decrease the needed safeguards. He argued that careful training was in itself a major precaution. He believed that superior training would yield the safety conditions necessary to protect U.S. sailors.

The Navy has always used real, shore-based reactors rather than simulators for training. One reason is Rickover's commitment not to send any reactor design to sea until it was fully proven. The training of Navy personnel and the testing of new reactors go hand in hand. Training is conducted in surroundings that replicate the ship environment. It includes work in real ship hulls, with all details correct. With the exception of the motion of the sea, the environments are identical.

The U.S. Navy provides an incredible amount of training to its personnel every year. The amount of technical manpower it takes to run all of the Navy's equipment on shore and at sea simply cannot be quantified. It is accepted, however, that the technical training given to people involved in nuclear operations is the best in the Navy.

The Navy has been operating hundreds of nuclear reactors for years under sea-going conditions. There has not been

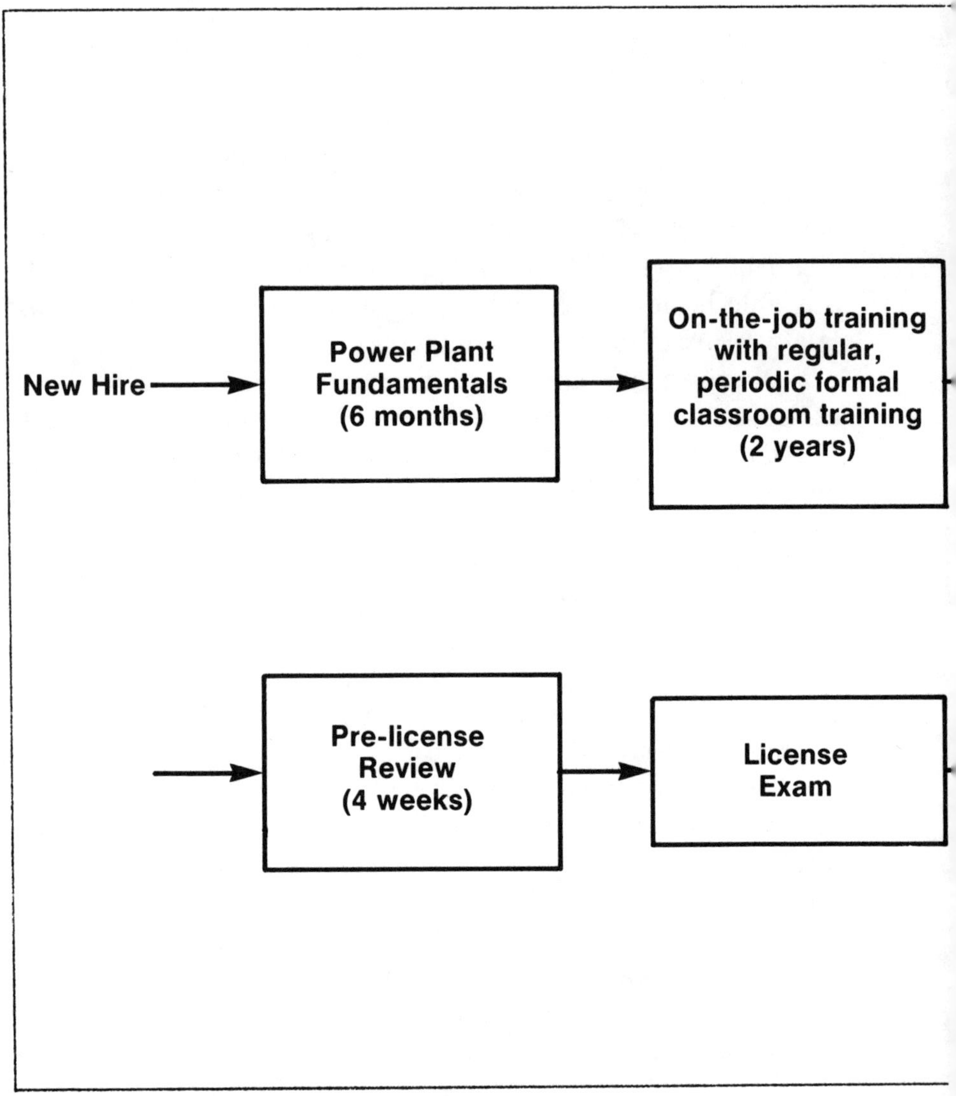

Figure 2. *Training Process for Nuclear Power Plant Operators*

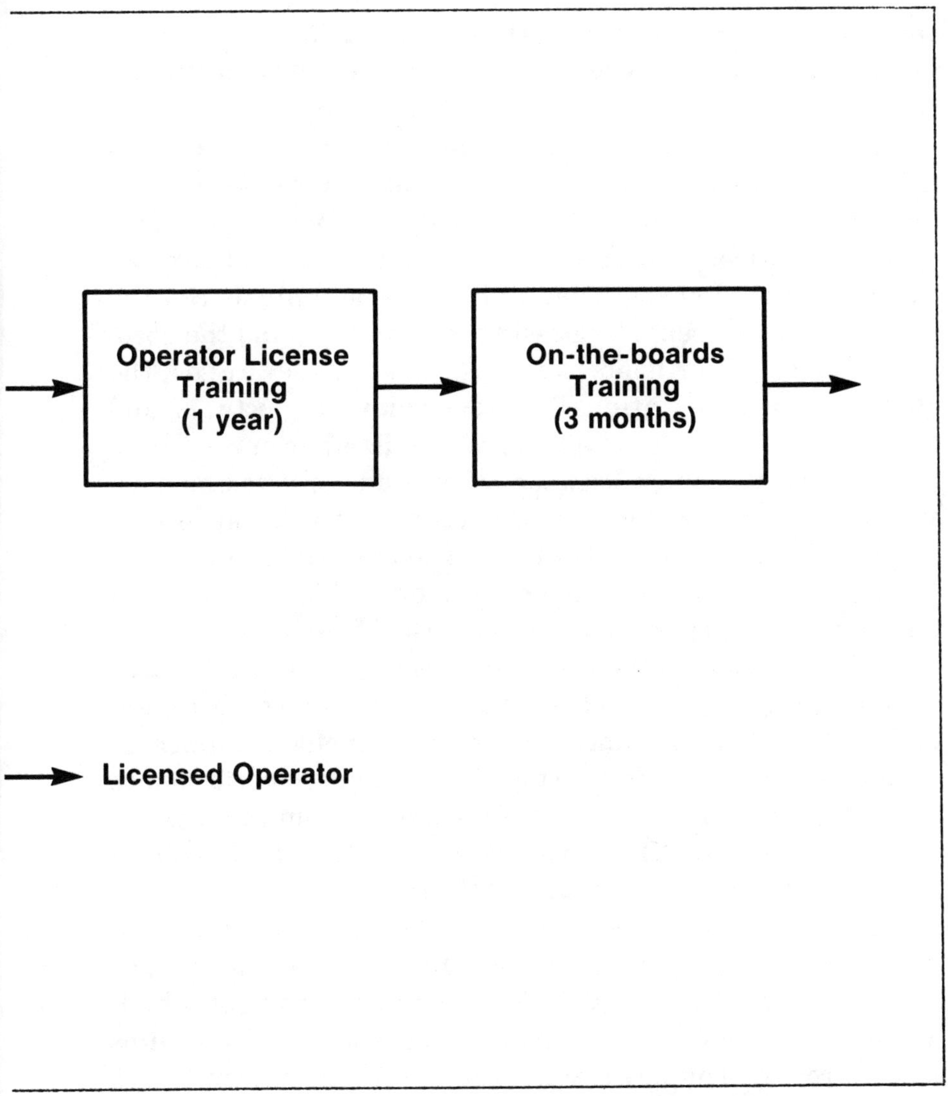

Courtesy of General Physics Corporation

one nuclear disaster involving those reactors. The most important components of that success are Navy training and maintenance procedures.

Nuclear personnel training differs from most other training in the Navy. It differs in intensity and degree of scrutinization. It includes extensive shore-based training, which is predominantly theory and procedures training, and is followed by ongoing training at sea. That, in itself, is not unique. But the exacting requirements for passing the training, and the absolute intolerance for nonperformance, are unique. At sea, the nuclear personnel continually attend seminars, lectures, and minicourses. This is not typical practice in other areas. There is far more interaction between officers and enlisted men assigned to the power plants than on other duty. The officers receive the same amount of training as do the enlisted men.

In some of the nonnuclear areas on a ship, a technician might simply do a performance checklist. The sense of urgency and critical nature of the work is not as high as in the nuclear area. But in the nuclear section, there are high levels of acountability for all performance. The training includes numerous evaluative exercises. Failure to achieve standard performance on the tests results in removal of the person from that assignment. Failure of the ship to achieve standard levels of performance on tests results in removal of the ship from service.

The commanding officers on nuclear-powered ships are the cream of the crop. They are well-trained in management as well as technical skills. A nuclear command provides a high level of visibility for the commander, and success in it ensures career growth. The key element in assessing performance is operation of the nuclear plant; therefore, the commander monitors that area most closely.

It will be useful at this point to profile another training company. General Physics Corporation was founded in 1966 by Dr. Robert W. Deutsch. As mentioned earlier in the chapter, regulation of the nuclear industry provided opportunities for independent training vendors. General Physics formed to help fill a vacuum in that area.

Revenue for General Physics in 1987 exceeded $114 million. Of this amount, approximately $30 million was generated by the Training and Technical Services Division. The GP Taurio Division, which contributed approximately $23 million, is involved extensively in training as well. GP Taurio specializes in services to the military, and the Navy is its major client.

The Training and Technical Services Division trains nuclear power plant operators at the utility site or in one of its own full-scale control room simulators. (It owns three.) It trains all control room personnel, operators seeking license qualification and requalification, and nonlicensed employees. In addition, it offers training to non-control room personnel such as maintenance, security, safety, and loss control technicians. The group develops customized training materials used to support simulator training. It uses everything from the most basic to the most advanced training technologies. It also sells training materials; a specialty includes utilities support.

GP Taurio develops training systems for the most modern ships in the Navy. It performs everything from job and task analysis to evaluation of the training. This includes design and development of curriculum and implementation of the programs. It has even designed a 520,000-square-foot Trident submarine training facility for the Navy.

General Physics is an engineering-driven company that has been extremely successful in delivering top-quality training and consultation. The scope of services it provides, in addition to training, arises from the sophisticated knowledge of its employees. I am pleased to see technology applied so well in support of training programs that enhance human performance.

In the training for commercial airline crews, as for nuclear power operators, there are federal regulations specifying minimum requirements for training and rechecking. The agency involved is the Federal Aviation Administration (FAA). FAA requires that captains be retested every six months and that first officers and flight engineers be retested yearly.

Commercial pilot training and rechecking can be done by an airline with its own training department or by outside vendors such as McDonnell Douglas. Some of the smaller airlines may rely on the vendors to do all their training and rechecking. Larger airlines usually do their own. However, airplane manufacturers always train commercial pilots on a new craft that is being added to a company's fleet because the manufacturers are the only parties with real experience on it. Airlines having their own training capacity will pick up the training for the new craft later.

To profile pilot training, I will refer to operations at the Pacific Southwest Airlines (PSA) Crew Training Center. The facility performs approximately 1,000 checkrides per year for pilots in addition to other crew-member training. Staffed with approximtely fifty people, the center houses classroom and simulator facilities.

PSA considers costs secondary to quality when training is involved. This is as it should be in a critical industry in which safety is Priority One. PSA decided to design its training to exceed FAA requirements. In addition to its DC 9 simulator, PSA also recently purchased and installed one of the world's most advanced commercial flight simulators, a British-built rediffusion model used to train pilots for the British Aerospace 146.

Most of the flight instructors are line captains who routinely fly the airplanes on which they provide training. This approach is taken because the captains all have up-to-date, hands-on experience with the craft on which they are instructing. Some flight instruction is done by check airmen who are also company pilots and have passed the FAA Instructor Training Program.

Training manuals are developed by the flight instructors using detailed specifications from the manufacturer. PSA's training philosophy seems to be, "Make certain that every detail is covered. Test for understanding and competency, and retest."

PSA puts much emphasis on screening applicants for pilot positions. Even so, the new employee training programs graduate only 90 percent of those who begin.

Initial training for PSA takes about three weeks. There are two weeks of ground school and another twenty-four hours on a flight simulator. There is continual testing and retesting throughout this entire period. The recurrent training consists of two days of ground school annually for all pilots, plus three simulator periods (four hours each) for captains and two simulator periods for first officers.

PSA invested $8-10 million in its new simulator, a substantial investment in training. However, if one compares the cost of operating a commercial airliner ($2,000/hour) with the cost of operating the simulator ($200/hour), one can see the return on investment.

The rediffusion simulator, when viewed from the outside, looks like an 18-by-20-foot steel box on four legs. The legs are hydraulic, jointed, and stand about twelve feet high. A person enters the simulator on a removable ramp from a second-story walkway.

Upon entering the box, one feels as if one has stepped into the cockpit of a British Aerospace 146, except that behind the pilot and first officer's seats are instructor seats and computer controls to operate the simulator. It is impressive to sit in the captain's chair and be surrounded by a real cockpit. The full-view visual system presents such a realistic perspective that one can easily feel as if the simulated trip is real. This is one feature that contributes to the exceptional fidelity of the simulator. FAA classifies it as a Phase III simulator, which is approved for all aspects of flight training

An interesting footnote: the simulator came from the manufacturer with a few visual scenes PSA felt it could use. It also has a built-in function with which one can program new scenes. The PSA training center simulator technicians created highly realistic scenes of airports and ground terrain that correspond to destinations of the airline. They not only obtain maps and flight charts, they also take many aerial photographs to use when creating graphics for simulator practice.

During the simulator training, 25 percent of the time covers normal airplane operation, the other 75 percent, malfunctions and emergencies. Pilots are trained and tested on literally every conceivable malfunction. Some of the emergency routines are drilled to allow perfect memory retention, because such situations would require instant response. Examples would be engine failure, decompression, or total electrical failure. Procedures for other potential malfunctions are trained to full competency but do not require memorization. Addressing them represents good judgment on the part of the instructional designer and training to the proper degree.

In addition to pilots, flight attendants use the training center for initial training and yearly rechecks. They receive classroom training and use fixed simulators to practice opening emergency doors and performing emergency evacuation procedures.

With a sincere commitment to high-quality training, an industry can accomplish almost anything. The thorough and rigorous training people undergo in the industries above sets an example for what can be achieved in human performance. In both the nuclear and airline industries, government regulations specify training standards. The industries treat those standards as the *minimum* requirements for their approach to training and tend to train well beyond them . . . something all company training managers should ponder.

Note: Since the time this chapter was written, Pacific Southwest Airlines (PSA) has changed its name to U.S. Air.

7

Astronaut Training

Astronaut training conducted by NASA at the Lyndon B. Johnson Space Center in Houston, Texas, may be the most elaborate training program in the country. It is well worth the reader's time to take an in-depth look at what may be the best high-tech training program anywhere.

Astronaut training today is training for the space shuttle, the centerpiece of the nation's space effort at this time. The shuttle flew twenty-four successful missions before the Challenger accident. In all those missions, the astronauts and ground crew displayed consistent excellence in performing their assignments. Based on the complexity of those missions and the extraordinary effectiveness of communications, we can certainly say that, in terms of training, they clearly knew what they were doing.

There are four crew position descriptions for the orbiter (shuttle): commander, pilot, mission specialist, and payload specialist. The commander and pilot are responsible for flying the orbiter. The mission specialist is the expert on the spacecraft itself and is trained to work with the payloads. Payload specialists are essentially passengers on board to operate scientific or other specialized equipment that performs research or gathers data. They receive approximately 2-3 weeks of flight training at NASA prior to a mission and do not participate in the elaborate training the other crew members receive.

Before examining the training, one should know about the prerequisites for shuttle crew candidates. *Pilots* must have a bachelor's degree in engineering, biological or physical science, or mathematics. They must also have a minimum of

1,000 hours pilot-in-command time in high-performance jet aircraft. Test flight experience is desirable. *Mission specialists* must have bachelor's degrees in the same areas as those for pilots plus three years' related experience. Advanced degrees are desired and can substitute for experience. *Payload specialists* are chosen by the company or agency sponsoring the payload on a particular mission. NASA is the final approval authority for payload specialists because it has ultimate responsibility for missions. Instructors and flight controllers also require extensive training. All training is tailored to the experience level of the candidates.

There are five levels of training. Level 1 is the most basic and uses training manuals and other self-study items. It familiarizes new candidates with NASA and the space program as it prepares them for further, more individualized training.

Level 2 reiterates the more important points from Level 1 and continues the depth of training by teaching the candidate the generic information needed to perform on a shuttle flight. Level 2 is more hands on than Level 1 and uses computer-aided instructional techniques.

Level 3 includes flight-specific training. It is the first point at which candidates are exposed to real one-on-one or one-on-two instructor training. In addition to continued classroom study, a Single System Trainer (STS) is used, capable of simulating any of the systems on an orbiter—for example, propulsion or flight control. The candidates learn one system thoroughly before going on to another system. Once a number of these single systems have been mastered, the necessary technical foundation has been established to proceed to the next level.

Level 4 involves the use of the Shuttle Mission Simulator (SMS). Through the use of the SMS, astronauts work extensively under conditions that closely approximate flight and mission conditions. The basis of the SMS is computer graphics and the ability to connect live to the mission control room. Using the SMS, astronauts practice everything they could encounter during an actual flight, from launch to space activities to landing.

Level 5 trains for specific flight and missions. Once the details of a flight are known, specific training on the particular operations required for that flight are learned. Training on this level is always associated with SMS activities.

For astronauts, the first three levels are much like a college curriculum. A training catalog lists over 5,800 separate lessons. The catalog identifies courses they need to pass for successful flight training. The center assesses their shuttle flying experience and determines how recently they have flown the shuttle, and categorizes their experience into six, twelve, eighteen, or twenty-four months. Based on the level of previous experience, matched with currency of flight experience, the remaining courses to be taken from the catalog are determined.

Because each crew is trained based on need, the catalog contains lessons for every aspect of flight. Examples of lesson titles are "Space Navigation and Orbital Mechanics," "Payload Extravehicular Activity Operations," "Generic Ascent Proficiency," "Deorbit Burn," and "Rendezvous Skills." Many of these lessons require or strongly recommend the use of the SMS.

The complex at the Johnson Space Center contains a variety of simulators used for various aspects of mission training. Regency CBT training is basically learning with a keyboard and CRT. It provides interactive lessons from the catalog of courses and allows trainees to make decisions and receive feedback on such topics as entry guidance and navigation.

The Orbiter 1G (1 gravity) trainer is a high-fidelity replica of the shuttle flight deck. It gives trainees early familiarization with the flight deck, making them aware of the location of panels, instruments, and controls. The Orbiter 1G also tilts to allow an experience of the launch position and practice of escape maneuvers from the vehicle.

Single System Trainers (SSTs) are medium-fidelity simulators. They are full-scale mock-ups of the flight deck with the exception that all of the panels and systems are not in place at all times. The simulator is set up based on the system to be learned. If the SST will be used to teach the navigation system, for example, the other control panels are covered. The trainee and instructor focus only on the system being learned, independently of the other systems.

KC-135 aircraft are specially modified for astronaut training. By flying the aircraft over a parabolic path, the effect of zero gravity is created. This effect lasts for about thirty seconds on each flight over the top of the parabolic path. During this time, astronauts practice using various types of equipment as well as eating or drinking in a weightless environment.

In addition to its use as a zero-gravity trainer, the KC-135 allows practice of approaches and landings, giving astronauts experience in handling a large aircraft.

The Weightless Environment Trainer is fundamentally a large swimming pool with a shuttle cargo bay submerged in it. The crew wears space suits in the pool, where there is a mock-up of the payload they will be handling on the mission, positioned in the correct location in the cargo bay. Water provides a realistic medium for this training because its viscosity and effect on motion closely reproduce the conditions of space. The Weightless Environment Trainer provides longer periods of weightlessness than are possible with the KC-135 training.

The Extra Vehicular Mobility Unit Simulator trains astronauts on techniques of operating the transportation pack they will use when working disconnected from the shuttle in space.

The Shuttle Mission Simulator Facility (SMS) houses the Fixed-Base Crew Station (FBCS), the Motion-Based Crew Station (MBCS), and the Spacelab Simulator (SS). This facility ultimately networks with Mission Control Center to perform the highest-order integrated simulations.

In order to support the simulators, the facility houses a computer complex containing thirty-two powerful and diversified computers. The computers not only control the simulators and the systems on board, but they also control the interface with instructor stations, operator stations, and Mission Control.

The Fixed-Base Crew Station is the only complete, high-fidelity simulated flight deck used in the training. It contains all of the controls and displays and, in every way, duplicates a shuttle flight deck. All of the controls and displays are active. Out of the window, scenes are provided by a digital image-generation system, so that the trainee can see images of what will actually be viewed during a real flight. Audio is also provided through hidden speakers in the simulator so that the sounds of the engine, launch, and booster rockets will be familiar during an actual flight.

As crew members near their flight date, they spend longer periods of time in the simulator—sometimes forty-eight hours or more. Astronauts have reported that the simulator experiences were so real that the flight seemed almost like another simulation. The Fixed-Base Station is used mainly for flight training and for payload bay training.

The Motion-Based Crew Station is also a high-fidelity simulator. It contains just the forward deck and is, therefore, smaller than the Fixed Base. It provides motion-based cues with which astronauts need to be familiar. All of the controls and instrumentation are active. The station provides an accurate simulation of launch, ascent, entry, and landing.

The Motion-Based Crew Station is mounted on a platform with hydraulic legs. It produces motion sensations the crew will experience when it performs particular maneuvers. During launch, for example, the platform is tilted 90 degrees. That positioning, combined with a series of motion subroutines, gives the crew members the impression of increased gravity. Visual and auditory cues are of high fidelity.

Both stations are supported by an instructor station and an operator station dedicated to that simulator. The instructor station is the "command center" for the simulator and is manned by an instructional team remote from the simulator. The instructors activate malfunctions and act as Mission Control Center during nonintegrated simulations. They also develop the simulation plan and evaluate crew performance. The operator station is where the technician or engineer who physically reprograms or reconfigures the simulator for each simulation works, and is located close to the simulator.

Flight controllers complete the first three levels of training following a program that is almost the same as that for the flight crew. Flight controller training is a certification program. Instructor training is also a certification program, somewhat different from the flight controller training. Instructors are former military jet pilots who have completed the certification program for instructors.

Integrated Simulations culminate the training program. During an Integrated Simulation, Mission Control Center and, later, the Payload Operations Control Centers are fully staffed by the teams that will ultimately support that particular flight. During these simulations, not only are the astronauts being trained, but the mission control team as well. In addition, at this stage indispensable relationships are being established between crew and ground control. The confidence and trust developed during Integrated Simulations are crucial to the team's performance, particularly in the event of abnormalities during a flight.

The Integrated Simulation is essentially a complete rehearsal of the planned flight, complete with payload activities. It can run from a few hours to several days. Throughout a session, every team's performance is evaluated, and anything questionable is scrutinized until the flight director is satisfied.

The crew for a planned flight is named from the pool of astronaut candidates. Once the crew is named, a training manager is assigned to it. The training manager and a core set of instructors will work on a dedicated basis with that crew until the flight is complete. In astronaut terms, they "ride with the crew the whole way." The team of instructors includes experts on propulsion, guidance, and computer systems, and a team leader. The team picks up the flight crew members the first time they enter a simulator as a crew.

Each person on a crew is individually evaluated by the training team. Individual training plans are developed for each crew member. All of the training plans are then integrated in an effort to ensure that a comprehensive crew-training strategy exists. The crew and the training team work on the training plan until everyone agrees with it. At that point, it is submitted to management, and a final plan is negotiated.

Once the plan is set, the training manager develops a detailed schedule of activities from that day forward to launch day. The schedule spells out everything the crew members will be doing, by day and by hour, for the next 1-2 years. The crew training plans, together with the certification plans for instructors and flight controllers, form the total curricula for mission training.

Intense SMS training begins approximately thirty weeks before the launch date. For approximately nineteen weeks, the instructor team and the crew work together on the simulators. Approximately eleven weeks before the launch date, Integrated Simulations begin. They continue until launch, which—it is to be hoped—is experienced by everyone as the "easiest simulation" of all.

Because Integrated Simulations are used to practice every possible malfunction or conceivable emergency condition, they are very active times. Crew and ground control work continuously to solve problems presented by the training staff. During a successful flight there would be a marked decrease in activity because malfunction would be rare.

The commitment to excellence in training at the Johnson Space Center is outstanding. Few of us will ever have the opportunity to experience a training situation as elaborate and expensive as this one. However, the center's commitment to and relentless pursuit of excellence is a model that can be emulated to enhance any training program.

8

Delivery Systems

The most visible part of a training program is its delivery. Delivery methods can range from one person's verbal explanation of how a job is done to hands-on training on equipment. When one considers that the equipment might be the helm of an aircraft carrier, one can appreciate the range of training possibilities.

In selection of the delivery system for a training program, many factors have to be considered, beginning with the goals of the program, and ending with feasibility studies on time, money, and equipment.

Training problems vary widely in type, complexity, and transfer requirements. The goal of one particular training effort might be to acquaint a class with a set of reference materials. For training of this nature, which simply has as its goal exposure to the material, class attendance might suffice as evidence of transfer. In contrast, a course in navigating a submarine into a particular harbor would require far more exacting criteria. The higher the complexity of the knowledge, and the higher percentage of knowledge transfer required, the more extensive the training criteria. This chapter will acquaint the reader with the process of identifying delivery systems and with the variety of options available.

There are a couple of widely accepted models used for making media selections. Through the use of a model such as the Reiser and Gagne, an instructional designer can effectively choose appropriate methodologies for training. The decisions will be based on such factors as what skill categories are involved, how much integration is required, and what risks result from non/poor performance.

Bloom's *Taxonomy of Educational Objectives* (1969, 1977) is a classic in the field of education. It presents a hierarchy of learning skills, setting down the order to use in introducing blocks of information in a curriculum. Bloom names six states: knowledge, comprehension, application, analysis, synthesis, and evaluation. By using the sequence, an instructional designer can ensure that fundamental information has been learned before introducing more complex information. The taxonomy can be summarized as follows:

1. *Knowledge:* basic recall of facts
2. *Comprehension:* understanding the nature of the subject
3. *Application:* use of rules and principles to solve a particular problem
4. *Analysis:* interpretation of information, recognition of implications and how the information is organized
5. *Synthesis:* creation of original ideas and concepts based on the information
6. *Evaluation:* arriving at correct judgments about a subject using all of the previous skills.

Most training programs include some form of lecture as part of the delivery system. The lecture is an appropriate choice when the goal is to provide facts organized conceptually for the listener. Lectures are useful in orienting a group to upcoming activities, or in adding facts to a listener's existing knowledge, or in demonstrating methods. Because lectures are the most common delivery system used in schools, most of us are very familiar with this teaching method.

Instructor-guided training is the most common type for the acquisition of psychomotor skills—driving a car, for example. It requires the integration of knowledge on both the intellectual and the hand-to-eye coordination level. Understanding must be translated into correct action. Instructor-guided training involves teaching individuals or small groups by leading them through a carefully supervised learning experience.

Higher-order cognitive skills, such as making fine discriminations and judgments, are also frequently taught using instructor-guided training. Almost all skilled jobs require this mode of teaching. It is difficult to imagine learning, without an instructor, how to operate a sailboat efficiently. It would be simple to learn, without an instructor or lecture, the names and functions of the components of the boat. However, sailing it is another matter. The variety of circumstances that can be encountered is nearly infinite. The instructor must, therefore, teach concepts and discrimination. The instructor transfers the "feel" of being at the helm—including, for example, how to interpret wave patterns to determine how they will affect the boat.

Instructor-guided training permits a wide range of student experimentation. For example, in an airplane designed as a training craft, with two sets of controls, an instructor can allow a great deal of flexibility as the student tries tactics and procedures which, although wrong, lead to learning what is right. Because the instructor can override the student's controls at any time, the student's experiments will not cause danger. The student discovers how it feels to perform correctly as a result of active problem solving. This method is very desirable because learning anchored in immediate *experience* is more likely to be retained.

Noninteractive media—such as video, films, slide-tape programs, audiotapes, and educational television—perform essentially the same function as that of the lecture. Although the method allows more opportunity to stimulate the learner visually and aurally, the learner still plays only a passive role. These media aids have some obvious advantages, such as availability, portability, information from experts, and the ability to present intricate concepts reinforced visually and aurally. However, merely showing a videotape or film, as an isolated activity, should not be considered true training.

Interactive media—such as live, two-way video, slide and audiotapes with workbook options, and computer games and exercises—can effectively provide certain kinds of training. When well-designed, these media combine the benefits of lecture with, to some extent, instructor-guided training. Even simple interactive courses require student participation. Training methods that require active responses from students are almost always more desirable than passive methods, especially for adult learners.

Using the interactive computer medium to train for the use of programs and applications for the same equipment is a natural choice. The transfer fidelity is virtually 100 percent because the student learns on the operational system he or she will continue to use. The other major asset is the trainer-programmer's ability to include in the exercises some branches, loops, and other opportunities for student feedback. "Branches" give a program flexibility to respond in different ways depending on the various possible answers from the student. In some cases, the computer can determine not only whether the answer is correct but also how quickly the student responded. The program can then present the most challenging sequence of instruction to the student who answers instantly, and a less demanding sequence to one who responds more slowly. It can also reexpose the student who missed the answer to the original sequence, or present an alternative explanation of the material. The medium has tremendous potential.

The quality of interactive computer instruction, however, depends on the quality of its design. For example, if a tutorial is supposed to instruct the learner on everything needed to use a program, it must be very carefully prepared. The tutorials typically accompanying hardware systems and software packages usually contain detail sufficient to suggest that the writers are extremely competent technically. However, one frequently gets the impression that the tutorials were developed by people lacking much background in instructional design or teaching. In addition, some learners drop from the ranks out of frustration with trying to figure out how to use the terminal and software. Much of this problem could be eliminated with more "learner-friendly" tutorial designs, which would require programming by people knowledgeable about educational techniques.

Interactive video resides in the same category as that for interactive computers. However, the addition of video is a quantum leap in terms of teaching options. To get a sense of that potential, imagine yourself at the movies watching an adventure. The woman on the screen is being chased by a ruthless killer through an empty factory. She comes to a corner where there is a window on the left, a staircase on the right, and a telephone (that may not work) on the wall. We can hear the killer, but he is not yet in sight. *You make the choice* as to what she does, and the movie proceeds according to your choice. If you chose the stairway, the woman is trapped in a sealed corridor and dies. If you chose the window, she moves out onto a ledge and buys more time. If you chose the telephone, it works—911 traces the call and the police arrive.

With that trip to the movies in mind, you can see that the possibilities of this teaching medium are limited only by creativity and computer capacity. This kind of software is now available for all but the most exotic training requirements. Limitations are more likely to come from training *budgets*.

At the most sophisticated end of the interactive media spectrum are simulators and live teleconferences. Teleconferencing allows audiovisual communication, via electronic broadcasting (usually by satellite), between people who are physically remote from one another. It can be used for "telecourses" or meetings, and allows participants (teacher and learner) to interact. Teleconferencing offers many benefits:

1. It can dramatically reduce the costs and inconveniences of frequent traveling. The Boeing Corporation reported a savings of 1.6 million travel miles between 1981 and 1986.

2. It provides greater access to technical experts. Many engineering-based industries conduct research and development at locations remote from their manufacturing sites. The ease of attending a teleconference on the work sites, as opposed to traveling, encourages more frequent exchanges of communication. It also decreases the time required to complete prototype designs because engineers and design teams in the field can "get together" on short notice.

3. Employees can keep up to date on the details of rapidly changing technologies by attending national seminars and conferences, such as those presented by the Institute for Electrical and Electronic Engineers (IEEE), the Association for Media Based Continuing Education for Engineers (AMCEE), and the National Technological University (NTU).

4. Employees have access to more educational opportunities—including training from instructors who may be 3,000 miles away. AMCEE alone offers over 400 courses from twenty-four schools. Hewlett Packard reported that 600 students using the Hewlett Packard satellite network attended an AMCEE course on Relational Data Base Systems.

This technology is becoming more and more popular. Estimated enrollment in teletraining courses during the 1984-85 school year was almost 400,000. During that time frame, there were about 10,500 courses offered on the air, and over 80 percent of the nation's colleges used video in some way for education. The Public Broadcasting System was the carrier for most of these courses.

Private-sector companies produce teleconferences, too. A good example is the popular annual conference on artificial intelligence offered by Texas Instruments.

The categories of teleconferencing can be conveniently broken into audio only, audio with graphics, and full-motion video. Audio teleconferencing (conference calling) allows people at several locations to participate in the same telephone call. With the appropriate equipment and audio bridge in place, audio teleconferencing can be clear and convenient and is the least expensive of the teleconferencing methodologies. It is appropriately used when the information to be discussed does not require visual references, as in a meeting to discuss a new policy.

Although many good products are available to support audio teleconferencing, one is of particular note for my purposes here. Individual Response for Analysis and Decisions (IRAD) is a product of the Logical Communications Co. of East Norwalk, Connecticut, that offers a special feature. The basic module, after registering participants onto the line, allows the moderator to poll the participants privately and simultaneously. Then the system automatically tabulates and summarizes the responses. The results help the moderator keep the discussion focused on the areas most relevant to the participants. The system also notes when a site has requested a follow-up question—sort of like electronically raising one's hand. The product has other capabilities and can be modified to specific needs.

Audio teleconferencing with graphics incorporates additional equipment into the telephone conference. An electronic blackboard is an example. When an individual at one location draws a diagram, it becomes instantly visible on a blackboard at the receiving end. The receiver can in turn transmit an image back. Facsimile slide projectors work like a copier except that the reproduction is digitized and reproduced at the receiving location. Freeze-frame and slow-scan videos provide a series of "snapshots" from one location to another. The effect is like that of watching a TV showing a series of slides.

Integrated desktop work stations appear to have tremendous potential for future information exchanges. Most allow the user to perform several types of computer applications simultaneously. For information exchange, some desktop work stations allow up to fifty users to share, among other things, text files, data files, and spreadsheet. Each participant with a work station is able to edit the information on the screen so that all other viewers can respond, not only via the audio link but also on screen.

Particularly exciting is the evolving capacity of these systems to incorporate video into the work stations. When the now-standardized Integrated Services Digital Network (ISDN) becomes more widespread in use, there will also be a greatly improved compatibility between systems from different manufacturers. Fiber optics, with their increased band widths, will accelerate the use of video information on these stations. Such telephone-line technology will replace some very expensive transmission media, such as satellites and transmitters. The principle is to digitize the video in the same way that voice and data are digitized for transmission today.

Audio with graphics is useful when visual aids are necessary, such as in discussions of engineering schematics, architectural drawings, or medical conditions. Although considerably more expensive than audio only, the inclusion of graphics is essential to some teleconferencing applications.

Full-motion video conferencing is the most complex and expensive of the options. It requires dedicated facilities, often specifically designed as a TV studio but arranged and decorated like a plush conference room. TV cameras, microphones, transmission equipment, and standby technicians are also generally required.

When visual contact with the other participants is necessary, full-motion video is the best way to teleconference. In any face-to-face meeting, people tend to observe one another's responses and body language. These cues can be important in achieving negotiation that is satisfactory to everyone.

Human factors are often a consideration in educational TV broadcasts. For example, when students enroll in a telecourse, the picture can give them a feeling of attending college. Teleconferencing allows students in remote locations to participate as readily as those in the classroom.

Live, interactive broadcasts are stretching media and educational technologies. So, too, are simulators. Mentioned previously in the context of pilot and nuclear power plant operator training, simulators represent the most sophisticated of the interactive media. When a training goal is to provide the learner with an experience that approximates the real task as closely as possible, simulators are the medium of choice. Physical fidelity, the exact duplication of the real equipment, is the goal of most simulators and tends to be what impresses the casual observer. However, *psychological* fidelity, accuracy of the learner's exposure to *performance* requirements of the job, is even more important.

Consider, for example, an operator learning a complex inspection task. The job involves judging the acceptability of a microscopic electronic circuit by looking at color, line widths, spaces, warps, and other defects. The actual job is done in a cleanroom, using a microscope. Physical fidelity—involving the cleanroom and microscope—is not critical at this point in training. In fact, the operator can better learn the complex structures of the device by viewing isolated portions of it first. This can be taught using a 35mm projector. The physical fidelity is distorted, but the psychological fidelity is good.

After the components of the device have been taught, the rest of the training requires the physical fidelity of a microscope and cleanroom. This exposure provides the experience of working with the sounds, smells, and surrounding activity levels typical on the job. During this time a trainer can help a learner build up speed and organize the work station.

To give the reader a perspective on a much more sophisticated system, I shall discuss the configuration of a generic multimedia flight simulator. The complex goals of the training call for a complex design. Suppose that the simulator being designed will be used to teach a complex set of responses that integrate advanced perceptual and cognitive skills and require judgments to be made in split seconds. Suppose that using the real equipment for training would be too costly and too dangerous. The training system must provide a medium for experts to interact directly with trainees. (The task could involve operational flights, weapons systems, combat, etc.)

To develop and refine perceptual skills, the training designers must first determine what visual references experts use in performing the tasks. These references must then be translated into a format, usually computer-generated graphics, presentable to a student in training. Extensive consideration goes into determining what should be included in the graphics, in order to achieve psychological fidelity. (There is also the constant challenge of creating the sense of a three-dimensional image with a two-dimensional medium.)

Graphics used must support and coordinate with the rest of the simulator. For example, an instrument panel with dials and digital readouts must provide information exactly in sync with what the trainee sees. The graphics and instrument panel are computer controlled.

The feeling of motion can be simulated by images moving in patterns designed to evoke that feeling. It can also be provided by actually mounting the simulator on a platform that maneuvers in sync with the images depicted on screen. Complex computer programming is required to achieve this.

To allow an expert pilot to give a trainee immediate feedback, an instructor station is built into the simulator. The instructor can activate preprogrammed simulator events or create new ones.

In a flight simulator, the student pilot should have a realistic experience result from any action he or she performs: if the trainee pushes the joystick forward, the platform should tilt to the appropriate degree, the dials and instruments should respond correctly, and the scenery should change accordingly. If the training is combat related, the images of targets or adversaries on the screen should move in a manner that precisely replicates what would happen in real warfare.

A simulator contains computer hardware and software, a physical environment, and visual, auditory, and motion systems. *Hardware* refers to the computer system that runs all of the programs in the simulation. *Software* is the set of instructions programmed into the hardware that enable it to perform the required functions. Hardware systems are mass produced, and only with the appropriate software can they perform different functions in the field. Simulator applications require powerful computers that can execute these programs at extremely high speed, in response to the trainee's actions.

The physical environment is designed to resemble as nearly as possible the surroundings involved in the actual task. For in-flight simulators, the environment is usually a cockpit fabricated on the same assembly lines that manufacture the real cockpit. They are, therefore, not identifiably different from the actual airplane the pilot will fly after training.

Visual systems on the real equipment can range from a CRT to a 360-degree, full-motion video screen. In a flight simulator, there might be a 270-degree screen that displays full-color, computer-generated graphics using a rear projection screen.

Audio systems are also included for aural integrity in the training. In the flight simulator, the trainee must practice frequent communications with air traffic controllers, other pilots, and the crew, as would happen in flight. This is accomplished through communication with instructors, simulated radio contact, computer-synthesized speech, and computer-controlled audio tapes.

The discussion in this chapter of teleconferencing and simulation is only a sketch, but it should give the reader an idea of the wealth of training opportunities afforded by these two high-technology methods.

Photo courtesy of Northern Telecom

An equipment technologist tests the wheel of a high-current ion implanter. After the wheel is loaded with wafers, it is spun up and scanned across an ion beam. The ions implanted in regions of the silicon wafers will alter their ability to conduct electrical current.

Photo courtesy of Northern Telecom

An equipment technologist programs a robot to transfer 150mm silicon wafers into a special furnace where they will be coated with "dielectric" layers.

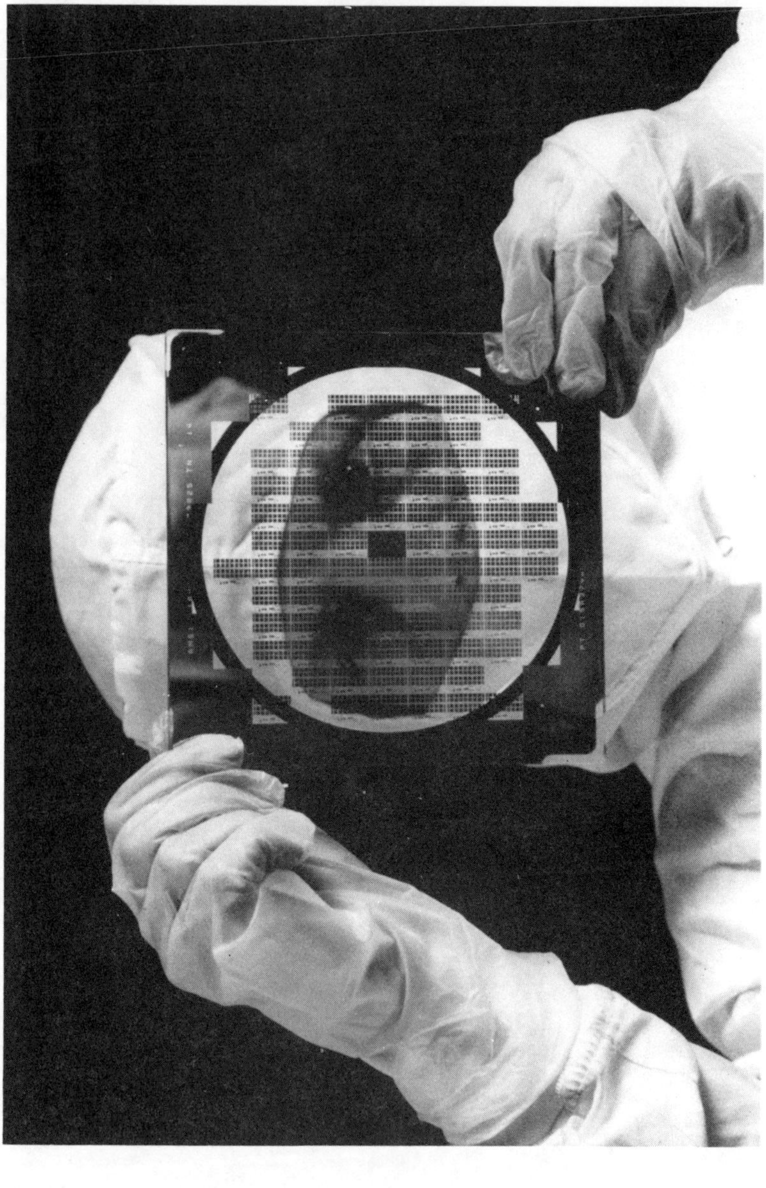

Photo courtesy of IBM Corporation

A glass mask containing images of IBM's 4-million-bit memory chip is examined by Paula Dema, a manufacturing technician at the company's semiconductor manufacturing and development facility in Essex Junction, VT. The mask is used in the manufacturing process that transfers circuit patterns to individual chips.

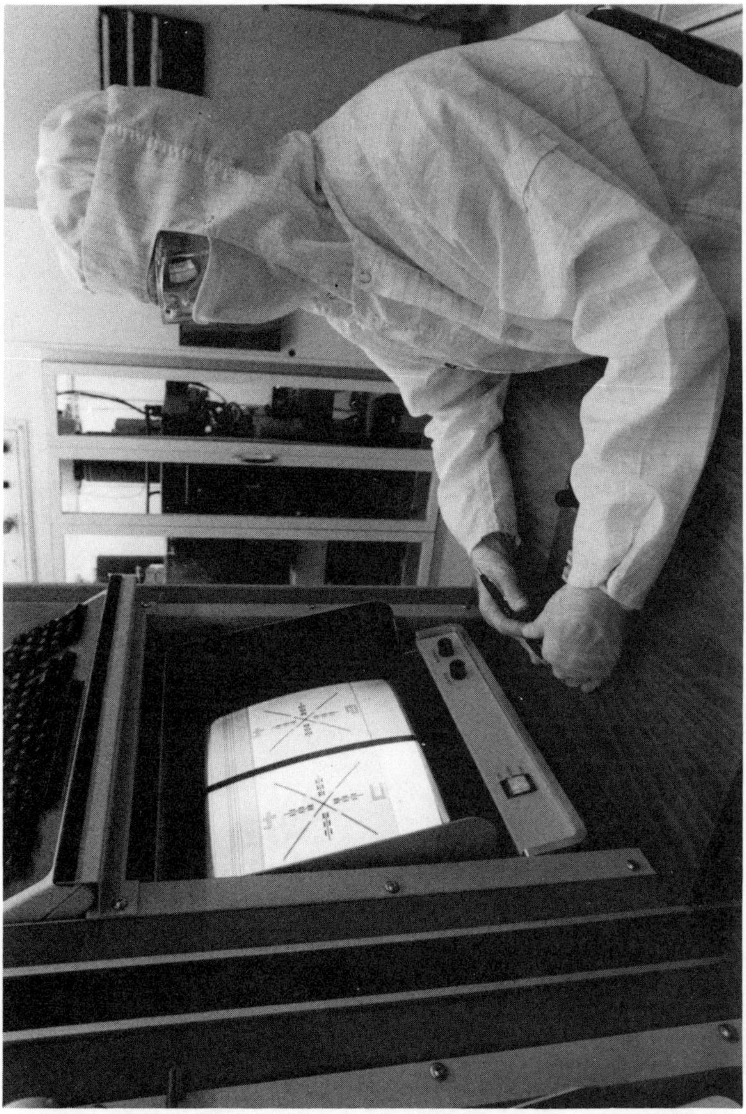

Photo courtesy of AT&T

An operator at the AT&T Bell Laboratories facility in Allentown, PA, works at a wafer stepper, which transfers circuit patterns to the silicon. This procedure is critical to all wafer processing.

Photo courtesy of Gatwick Road Crawley

Rediffusion Simulator, British Aerospace 146

Photo courtesy of National Aeronautics and Space Administration

A view of part of the flight deck of the Space Shuttle Orbiter 102 Columbia

Photo courtesy of National Aeronautics and Space Administration

Finalists in NASA's Teacher in Space Project get their first experience of micro-gravity aboard the KC-135.

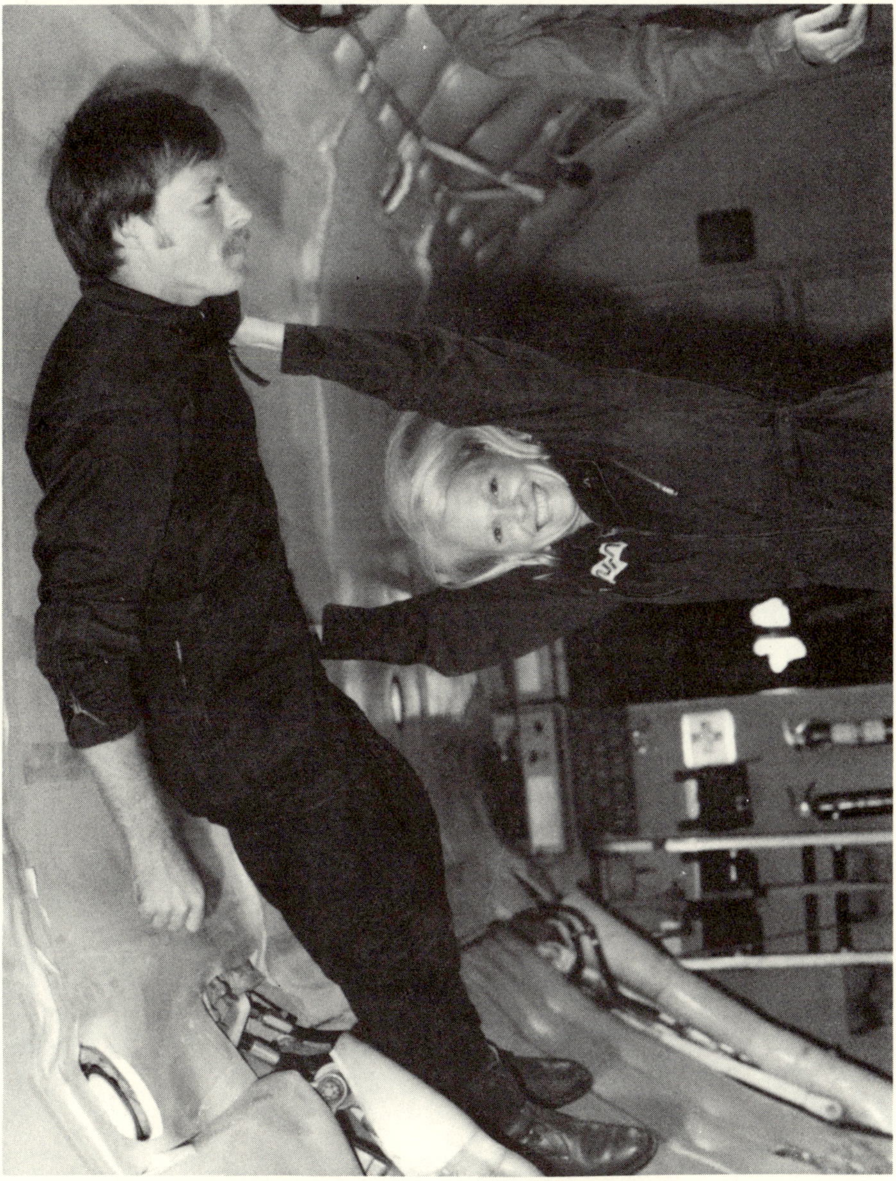

Photo courtesy of National Aeronautics and Space Administration

Astronauts in zero-gravity training aboard the NASA KC-135 aircraft used for zero-g simulations.

The weightless environment test facility is a 25-foot-deep pool used for training and engineering evaluation of in-space procedures with NASA hardware.

Photo courtesy of National Aeronautics and Space Administration

Astronauts practice extravehicular chores in the submerged mock-up that simulates the weightlessness of space.

Photo courtesy of National Aeronautics and Space Administration

The single-system trainer simulates the flight deck but exposes the student only to the particular system being studied at the moment. For the system under study, real equipment is in place and operating; cardboard replicas fill in the spaces for the other systems.

Photo courtesy of National Aeronautics and Space Administration

Photo courtesy of National Aeronautics and Space Administration

An exterior view of the Johnson Space Center's Shuttle Mission Simulator.

Photo courtesy of National Aeronautics and Space Administration

A mezzanine-level view of the Fixed-Base Shuttle Mission Simulator

A computer-generated scene depicting astronaut Joseph P. Allen IV latched onto the Palapa communications satellite during retrieval operations for the first of two spacecraft. The space shuttle Discovery waits nearby.

Photo courtesy of National Aeronautics and Space Administration

9

Winning Training Strategies

Numerous considerations determine training strategy. Many of them have already been discussed. This chapter will summarize them and then describe their application.

The importance of *thorough planning* has been a major theme throughout this book. It should be established by a company's top management, which should retain ownership for and commitment to the plan even though implementation requires delegation throughout the entire organization. The long-range training plan has such serious implications for a corporation's success that accountability and visibility at all levels, but especially the top, are appropriate.

Analyzing the company's *business plan* is another step in developing a training strategy. It is very appropriate to ask questions, verify assumptions, and probe into portions of the plan that are unclear. Simply reading the document will not suffice. A training strategy well-grounded in the business plan can be effectively targeted and focused.

Previous chapters have discussed the future of manufacturing and how jobs might change. It apears fairly certain that the most critical skills shortage will be in technician skills on the factory floor. The reader has been exposed to some techniques for training that population.

The scientific techniques and technology of today can more than adequately support any training need. When training must be perfect, it can be. This book has shown that the conscientious execution of a good training strategy pays off in having the right people in the right places at the right times. It has also been shown that specialized instructional techniques tailored to particular groups greatly enhance training effectiveness.

But it is the *follow through* on training strategy that separates the winners from the losers in worldwide industrial competition. Most executives probably know their company's business plans and how to create substrategies from them. The real challenge lies in *implementation*. This chapter will explore that all-important step.

The string that ties strategy to successful implementation is *human interaction*. To create the conditions for successful implementation requires far more than issuing regular memos and reports. It calls for team building, networking, creating timelines and milestones, disseminating information, "buying in," and developing accountability mechanisms. If the "people" element is not cultivated, the rest of the effort is wasted.

Buy-in is a key concept. There must be a sense of ownership and enthusiasm for the training programs if they are to succeed. Many routes can be used to achieve buy-in; the most common is employee involvement. When people feel as though they have participated in building a project, they tend to nurture it, take a personal interest in it, and feel proud of it.

The senior-level person responsible for training can use regular meetings to elicit opinions and suggestions from other top staff members. Ongoing progress reports keep the training effort visible at the senior level and foster ownership. A golden opportunity to promote buy-in arises during the data-collection phase. While a manager analyzes the organization for potential training opportunities, he or she can have discussions with the many individuals who provide the data. Because this data gathering tends to cross all organizational divisions, a manager can generate a lot of employee interest—and buy-in—during this phase of planning.

During my first meeting with the vice president of an electronics company, I asked to see the corporate business plan. My request raised concern about how I would use the information and why I needed it. I explained how developing a proactive training strategy required an in-depth understanding of the company's goals. Once this became clear, I received the documents. (Naturally, I had to sign nondisclosure forms.) The VP was very interested in what would result from my analysis. He provided me with key contacts in all of the manufacturing plants. We also agreed that he would participate in this process: it would not be merely his delegating and my reporting.

The next important stage was attracting the interest of the plant managers. We talked this over and decided that the VP himself would explain most of the process to the group. As we prepared for the presentation, made at an operations review, the VP learned more and more about my approach. He did a good job of describing the data I would be collecting and its potential uses. The group appeared impressed. By the time I began to answer questions, the atmosphere was very congenial.

Plant managers in most companies have a great deal of authority and responsibility. They do not simply sit in meetings, nod their heads, and agree to things just because the presenter is a vice president. I, therefore, felt encouraged about our start because I had hoped for receptivity and found it.

The next step was individual meetings with the plant managers at their home factories. The choice to meet at their factories resulted in a lot of travel for me. However, it was the only realistic option for this kind of data gathering. At this point I began to get a feel for each factory and its product lines, and people began to see me and get a sense of who I was. The early meetings were mainly for listening and learning. However, I also took this opportunity to continue educating them about my process of analysis. Each plant manager was eager to see my findings. and some even wanted to help sort the data.

For the sake of expediency, I will now focus on one factory to illustrate my point about cultivating buy-in during early data gathering. The plant manager played a role similar to that of the VP in the operations review.

This factory operated twenty-four hours a day, seven days a week, and held three routine meetings once a month. That meant attending meetings at 6:30 a.m., 9:00 a.m., and 11:30 p.m. There was no question in my mind that the factory had a 24-hour culture, and I had to flow with it if I was going to get the acceptance I needed. At these meetings I explained the data-gathering plan and was introduced to everyone in the plant. I spent almost two weeks in the plant. I attended several meetings, but I collected the best data one on one.

The engineering manager had a tremendous collection of data on products. Apparently, few people had serious interest in all the data he had so carefully collected. He willingly spent all the time it took showing me his work and answering my questions about it. He had yield charts from years back on mature products. He had graphs and pie charts that analyzed defects and trends in defects. He also had some unique data on how specific processes operated on particular pieces of equipment.

A cost analyst in the finance group turned out to be another source of invaluable information (not surprising). She had extensive reports on the costs of everything. She knew the value of one yield point on any product. She had curves that projected the impact of improved yields, which showed extraordinary opportunities for profit on some of the products. She had figures broken down, such as the dollar value produced per operator on a monthly and annual basis. She, too, was more than willing to help. In fact, she seemed almost relieved that someone had finally taken serious interest in her work.

My meetings with the manufacturing personnel were exciting. I began to feel the hum and throb of the engine. These were the people in direct contact with the work. I not only looked at reports and data in their offices, I also spent all the time I could on the factory floor. I would meet an equipment technician and hear the minute details of a piece of equipment that was more finicky than Morris the cat. The people could tell I liked them, and most took an interest in my work.

The people on the factory floor were especially interested when I mentioned training. Most of them felt they needed more, so I was careful not to raise any false hopes. I emphasized that I was collecting data that *their management* would use to learn more about *possible* areas for training. Anyone who has worked on a shop floor knows that the grapevine makes it extremely easy to create wrong impressions and misinformation with casual remarks. Because credibility is an absolute necessity in data gathering, I was very clear about my work and avoided raising expectations. If I had been perceived as having made a promise and not fulfilled it, cooperation would have been difficult or impossible during implementation.

When I had finished the data gathering and sorted it, I had a series of meetings with the factory staff. We looked the data over, and we questioned, challenged, and probed until it began to make sense to everyone. At this point it became apparent that some of the data had implications for that plant, and we focused on organizing it further. There were other data that looked important, too, but seemed to call for examination by the vice president and other plant managers.

The presentation at the next operations review generated a great deal of discussion. There was just too much to say, and other business had to be conducted at the meeting. The group decided to stay for another half-day to continue discussions. The vice president was being conscientious about keeping his peers informed. I was pleased: I had buy-in of the first order. At this factory, the management decided to design and implement a training and certification program for operators. I assisted in selecting a training manager and helped get things off the ground.

A major change in focus occurs between the data stage and implementation. At this point there is the transition from buy-in to commitment. Choices must be made for target areas for the first training programs. Project planning begins in earnest, as timelines and resources are identified.

Collecting and analyzing data can be tedious work, but envisioning the future customer satisfaction that will result can be rewarding. When potential opportunities for improved performance arise, manufacturing people get enthusiastic. In fact, they are likely to want to grab the information and charge off with it. They will probably start writing up training schedules before you have finished your presentation. Therefore, it is important to strike a balance between planning and activity at this point, to harness that energy and enthusiasm without stifling it.

It is time to educate people further. Working with the resources supporting the training effort, do a decision analysis. Take several important performance criteria, and apply them to the choice of a training program. You will want to select a project that supports the main indicators of the company and the factory involved. You want a high dollar payback for the investment and should choose a goal that is easily measurable.

It is also important you make sure people understand what is involved in the process of designing and developing training materials. The people who are now your resources will probably remain closely involved in the development of the programs. You may have to teach them how to create training programs step by step.

The decision about how to attain the needed training materials will be made based on many factors. The major considerations are: how soon are the materials actually needed, are there people inhouse who could produce them, are they available, and which method is the most cost effective?

Using outside training experts has its pros and cons. On the one hand, you can expect high-quality materials and relatively short production time. If you locate people who are expert in the particular field for which you are developing the program, you may be acquiring additional field expertise as well as program development expertise.

On the other hand, even with the most highly experienced outside consultants, you cannot expect to just hire them and then forget about things until the programs are complete. You need to specify what you need up front. You should have a formal contract drawn up specifying all of the expectations on both sides, to avoid future disappointments. If you do this and review progress regularly, you should get what you expected.

Outside people are not familiar with the ins and outs of your company, so be prepared to help them from time to time. You should try to familiarize them with your company's culture so that they can avoid major mistakes.

In other words, with outside training experts, "Let the buyer beware." Do your homework and check up on the company or individual(s) you hire. In this way you can avoid the most serious mistake: hiring someone who cannot do the job.

Outside experts can be expensive but, depending on your needs, cost effective in terms of time saved on the project. If you have a distinct methodology in mind for your materials, be sure that the outside experts agree they can work with your system. Sometimes they have their own way of doing things and may not have the flexibility to use your system.

The only other drawback is the lost opportunity to develop some of your own people's program development skills.

Using inhouse staff to develop programs also has its pros and cons. You can foster a sense of ownership (buy-in) more effectively by having your own people build the program. Inhouse people might be more successful in improving processes when they get a chance to participate in program development. They also get an opportunity to learn the skills of program development. In addition, maintaining materials generally is less of a problem if the originators are inhouse employees.

On the other hand, using inhouse resources has drawbacks. If the original commitment of resources to work on the program is not "cast in concrete," priorities may change during the project. I have seen this happen. It is frustrating for the project coordinator and demoralizing to the person who is learning instructional design for the first time.

Another drawback is that program development will take considerably longer if your inhouse resources are learning on the job. You are vulnerable to unexpected turnover as well; for example, if employees are transferred or promoted, they may not be able to complete their project.

With proper supervision, you can produce training materials of respectable quality. If you use inhouse resources, you may find the following guidelines helpful.

Your staff will learn how to perform task analysis—detailed study of the job identified for training. The task entails—you guessed it—data gathering. But now the data pertain to specific job requirements. What are the skills and knowledge needed to perform the job? What are the steps involved? In a complex job, this analysis can require extensive flow charting.

Expert analysis is the fine tuning of the task analysis. In this phase, the training designer, using a variety of techniques, learns from experts the best method for doing the job. This valuable information largely determines the program's potential.

Next, the training designer sets course objectives, followed by more detailed objectives for the learning segments. Media are selected, such as workbooks, video, slides, programmed instruction, simulation, computer-assisted instruction, or whatever best suits the training objectives.

Finally, the content of the program is established. Sometimes the people working directly with you can write the courses; in other cases they will coordinate the input of experts in the company. The content is continually reviewed in draft form until it is perfect and ready to be used in training.

The people not involved in the course development have essentially been waiting all this time. This is a precarious phase because of the time lag between the initial enthusiasm from the staff and the beginning of training. Therefore, be sure to keep the staff apprised of the progress on course development, instructor training, and other behind-the-scenes activities.

Before formally implementing the training, make sure everyone understands what they are committing to in terms of time and resource allocation. Capacity plans should have training times factored into them, to allow people to follow through on their training to completion. On the factory floor, training often calls for hands-on use of actual production equipment. If this activity is not carefully planned and coordinated with everyone affected, serious problems and bad feelings can result.

Another example of a program successfully implemented using these principles involved training engineering technicians. Essentially, the project entailed providing engineers with assistants working directly for them. The assistants were technicians who could run experiments and handle details that freed the engineers to do other work.

An analysis of the group showed a wide disparity in the range and depth of skills. Structured observations and interviews revealed that many of the people assisting the engineers were not able to perform to expectations. Since these positions frequently were promotional opportunities for operators, engineers were obliged to select the best applicants from the available work force.

The project was challenging because the jobs were relatively unstructured. Each engineer had a different set of requirements, and the technicians numbered in the hundreds. Data analysis revealed the various skills and knowledge needed in the job, which were then studied to determine which would be the most valuable targets for training.

Applying the instructional design procedures previously discussed, the company developed a course. It basically taught beginning engineering skills and focused on the processes specific to the job. The course content was developed with extensive input from engineers throughout the company.

To accommodate the wide variations in jobs, the company built a mentoring component into the program. This feature created a new opportunity for engineers to teach, in a structured way, details they wanted their technicians to know. It also compelled the engineers to take the time to think carefully about what they really wanted. The program also provided methods for effectively communicating these goals.

The program succeeded in many ways. Test scores showed significant increases in skills and knowledge. Factories showed improvement in their processing and attributed much of it to the training. Engineers had enough time freed up to allow them to devote more energy to solving processing problems. Morale improved dramatically. Both engineers and technicians felt that communication had improved considerably.

There is a macro training strategy it would be useful to discuss at this time. Although I have never had the opportunity to implement it in its purest form, I consider it very practical for many reasons. The strategy is based on the assumption in a company culture that training is a part of everyone's job. Under that company ethic, employees would expect that on some occasion(s) during their employment, they would be asked to train other workers. Everyone who spends time in the role of a trainer learns the subtleties of communicating complicated information. After returning to their regular job, they will benefit from the training skills they have learned. Furthermore, as the common axiom says, "If you want to learn a subject well, teach it to others." By teaching a subject in which we are knowledgeable, we push the limits of our knowledge. Therefore, training develops a person's knowledge as well as communication skills.

The beauty of such an approach is that it builds tremendous flexibility into a company. One difficult problem training managers face is staffing: most frequently, there is a shortage. Requests for training frequently exceed the capabilities of the existing staff. This makes the strategy of marshaling the resources of the existing employee base most sensible. If the training is needed urgently, the management will reallot employee time to accomplish it.

A major mistake by a training manager is overstaffing. If a large training staff is hired to meet a one- or two-year training demand, difficulties arise when the need subsides. Furthermore, during economic downturns, a large training staff may be trimmed back, sometimes to the point of destroying its effectiveness. A company can lose years of investment in building content expertise.

However, if the company had kept the training staff small all along and worked to develop the employees temporarily assigned to training, the company would retain more of its expertise. A "lean" training staff used effectively can withstand economic downturns far more successfully.

Another strategy, particularly relevant to equipment, is called "embedded training." With this technique, a training program is designed and built into the equipment. Any piece of equipment with a computer as part of its construction can have embedded training.

A simple example is the tutorial that comes with a personal computer. Some of these lessons are designed so that the first time an operator uses the computer, that person must perform a preprogrammed sequence that gives instruction on key aspects of the machine's use. This method helps manufacturers avoid excessive troubleshooting inquiries from new owners who have not carefully read the instruction booklet. Embedding the instructions into the equipment helps eliminate this problem.

If you consider that the Pentagon purchases expensive and complex systems regularly—ships, airplanes, land vehicles, missiles—embedded training makes sense. In this case, however, it may not be a simple exercise for a first-time operator, but an entire subsystem dedicated to training.

A surface ship or submarine has combat system teams, which might consist of a sonar technician, a fire-control technician, a ship-control technician, and an officer. Each technician must be extensively trained on the equipment. Because communication is critical during a battle, teams need opportunities to practice communication under conditions that simulate real battle.

In the training mode, all of the equipment in a combat system must work together. When the ship controller changes course, the sonar technician should get corresponding readings. Fire control must get feedback on effectiveness in reaching targets. The whole practice is a computer-controlled simulation.

Frequently, the equipment on board has to be retrofitted for training capability. Equipment, such as sonar systems, is much more versatile when high-quality training programs are built into it. Not surprisingly, the concept of embedding training into systems is becoming popular with defense contractors and procurement agencies.

Of course, embedding a system does not inherently equal high-quality training. Management must ensure as high a level of quality for the training program as for the system itself.

It's customary today for a defense contractor to include training in the purchase contract for a system. Unfortunately, the training is usually then handed off to the training department, which is typically excluded from the contracting process and not kept adequately informed of design revisions or even contract revisions. Insufficient emphasis is given to the role training plays in the system's ultimate success in the field. Government procurement agencies and contractors should be aware of this problem. Training is not something to be merely crossed off a contract adherence checklist: it is critical to the success of the venture.

A secondary but strategically indispensable benefit of implementing training programs is an organization's improved overall ability to train and be trained. Well-designed programs enhance company culture. For example, they promote flexibility and give people the confidence that they can learn new job assignments and succeed in them.

Readiness for change is an asset to today's fast-paced, high-tech businesses. But to change company emphasis from job security and longevity to challenge and change requires more than good training programs. This is where the expertise of organizational development (OD) specialists can be important.

OD specialists hold a global view of their organizations; therefore, they can provide valuable support in the implementation of programs. In many organizations, an OD may function on a different plane from that of the technical training folks. It is a waste of resources if these groups pass like ships in the night. Each has a natural contribution to make to the other's efforts.

If the OD group spends its time almost exclusively with the top brass, it loses its effectiveness as a contributor. On the other hand, an OD group that gets involved in the details of the company's mission can enhance day-to-day planning and be a tremendous asset.

It may appear easier to some readers to work through technical issues without involving the OD. In fact, I have seen environments in which the OD group slowed progress for no apparent reason. However, I have also seen environments in which the ODs worked in sync with management and technical training people. In that case, the cohesiveness of the effort produced results far superior to what any of the groups could have accomplished separately.

There is no substitute for professionalism in any field, including training. Too many companies use the training positions as convenient repositories for people they don't want in "important" jobs. I have seen this tactic used at levels from line worker to vice president. This attitude reflects a sorrowful lack of understanding of the importance of training.

It requires special knowledge to design the best training department, or to manage the training program. It also requires special knowledge and ability to perform training on the line or in the classroom. There are many things to consider when staffing a training position. First and foremost, management must take the position seriously, then analyze what is needed and determine some criteria before throwing people's names into a hat.

Education and experience are primary considerations. Does a person's work history include serious experience with training? I have met excellent training managers who worked their way up in a factory to senior management positions. They were effective, capable people who had kept an open mind and learned as they worked. But I have more often met successful training managers who steered their education toward training and brought some valuable theory and knowledge into the work place with them.

There are degree programs in instructional design, educational technology, training and development, media and industrial psychology, to mention a few. If you ask candidates who attended programs like this about their courses, you can learn a lot about the curricula.

Training is a profession, not just a job. Each company has to decide whether it is seeking a professional or merely filling a slot. Salary levels may have to be rethought, but the effort is worthwhile.

The job of line trainer is usually performed by a present or former operator. This position must also be well thought out. You cannot expect to find the type of training professionals discussed above in these jobs. However, you can teach and instill professionalism. People who are selected for training jobs on the factory floor should be the best available. They should not only possess the best skills but also have the best attitudes and work ethics.

For a training program, the line is the place where the rubber meets the road. Fine expertise and design are useless if they can't be used the way they were intended. The trainers have to be strong enough to deflect peer pressure aimed at lowering the standards of the training. It is not unusual for trainers to work extensively with resistant or incapable workers. The job requires patience and perceptiveness. Trainers on the line are usually dedicated people and deserve as much support as can be provided.

A winning training strategy goes one step beyond successful implementation of a good program. It makes a positive, cost-effective contribution to the company. It follows up on implementation. Measuring and reporting the results of training complete the picture. If everything has been researched and planned properly, the results fall easily, like fruit from a tree. Company sponsors should be kept supplied with this fruit. They need it to verify not only what the training manager has accomplished, but also what they have accomplished.

Readers should now understand what is involved in a training strategy. If so, they will be prepared to deal with the training needs of a business. Applying even a few of the ideas discussed in this chapter should significantly enhance plant start-ups and the introduction of new product lines.

10

Industrial Humanism

U.S. corporations are growing more aware of people as individuals. They are beginning to build work environments with facilities that support aspects of employees' lives that are not directly connected to their jobs (such as on-site day care). They are beginning to develop programs and policies that nurture rather than punish. For both practical and ethical reasons, industry is becoming more humanistic.

A happy and healthy employee is more likely to be productive. A healthy employee is also far less expensive to the company in terms of medical care and absences from work. Recognizing this, some companies have made fitness facilities available to their employees on site.

A model "humanistic" company is Rolm Corporation in Santa Clara, California, which has provided generously for its employees in various ways that demonstrate consideration and encouragement of employees as individuals. Early on, the company committed itself to attracting the best people. The intense competition for talent in Silicon Valley makes it desirable to plan a business complex that offers employees as much comfort, convenience, and nurturance, if you will, as possible. Rolm's company culture is energetic and fitness oriented. The Rolm staff, at work and play, is committed, hard working, and hard playing. Rolm's environment shows that the company not only wants the best people but also expects to treat them accordingly.

Rolm has a staff of professionals assigned to the fitness center. The facilities include a large indoor/outdoor pool, full-size basketball court, exercise rooms and equipment, handball courts, and a jogging/fitness track on the company grounds. These facilities are available to all employees and their families.

In addition to the health center, Rolm provides a luncheon facility that rivals most hotel restaurants. The environment is pleasing architecturally, with split levels of tables and booths, plants, and fancy filament lighting overhead. The variety of food selection accommodates the most individualistic of tastes. The facility features a grill, a health food bar, a hot luncheon line, a soup and salad corner, and a small bakery.

When visiting Rolm, strolling through the greenery and fountains between buildings, one gets the impression that top management chose to make a clear statement: "We care about your health and your comfort, and we are going to *show* you we do."

Corporations are becoming more interested in families as well. Some provide day care on the premises. Others actually *encourage* paternity leave of up to three months after a child is born. Health benefits for family members can be generous. It is not unusual for manufacturing plants to hold elaborate open houses so that friends and families can see where employees work and what they do. Such activities recognize the importance of a person's life off the job. The appreciation of significant stages in a person's family life signifies a growing enlightenment and sensitivity at corporations.

Education is another area of opportunities for employees. Most companies offer some reimbursement for education. They support education as a means for employees to pursue their own development and require only that the educational program be somehow related to the person's work or future career goals. This benefit reinforces the mutual commitment between company and employee. The more generous this company benefit is, the more clearly the company conveys the message that it values education. It also demonstrates trust in the employees' own wisdom and ability to make decisions for themselves.

Personal support programs pay for such services as counseling, weight control, habit control, and drug and alcohol programs. These services make still another important statement to employees: "It is human nature to have personal problems, and we want to give you the best possible opportunity to resolve them." Such services can help companies retain experienced employees it may have taken months or even years to develop in expertise. Furthermore, these services show the company's compassion for and commitment to its employees. Confidentiality is usually carefully protected in connection with such programs. They give managers a fair and caring way to deal with employees who get into trouble. If people choose not to avail themselves of these benefits, they have to take responsibility for the consequences.

Such programs and facilities can show employees that management regards them as important.

Another approach, in some ways more profound, is to foster meaningful work and working relationships. Ten years ago, the profession of organizational development (OD) (mentioned in previous chapter) was limited to a small group of people. It was regarded as a somewhat esoteric discipline by many top managers. Today, however, attitudes have changed. The bookstores are brimming with volumes on how to redesign or reinvent corporations. Corporate leaders reading these books seem to be taking the message seriously. In their drive to become more competitive, they are becoming more willing to try new ideas on larger scales than ever before.

Organizational development specialists are trained to look for ways to influence organizations to be more flexible and make changes as needed. The job of a professional agent of change is akin to corporate therapist: the roles of family therapist and OD are very similar. Both analyze people in relation to systems. The main difference is the scale of the interventions and the fact that ODs worth their salt are able to understand and facilitate not only all of the business aspects of the intervention but also the interpersonal ones. Peter Block (1981) states:

> Whether your client is a family or an organization, politics is affecting people's behavior and their ability to solve problems. Your task as a consultant is to understand enough about the politics of the situation to see how it will affect your project and the implementation of your recommendations. Too often we collude with the client in pretending that organizations are not political but solely rational.

Being a professional agent of change often means putting people in uncomfortable positions in order to stimulate change that improves the company's performance. A major part of that activity is to highlight the dynamics of how departments or individuals interact. The execution of a good business plan requires cooperation and teamwork. Relationship problems and/or structural problems greatly inhibit the ability of any group to perform. This effect is magnified in larger companies and contributes significantly to productivity problems. But when people have a commitment to a vision, to their company, to one another, and to themselves, they rarely fail.

Living organisms, by nature, strive for equilibrium. Change is always uncomfortable since, by definition, it is a movement away from equilibrium. However, without change, an organism cannot grow or evolve and so must die. Applying that analogy to a corporate environment, one can see that evolution in the right direction enables a corporation to survive, grow, and thrive.

Besides making people painfully aware of their problems, ODs help them resolve those problems. They use a variety of methods and techniques—ideally, in support of an overall strategy—including individual one-on-one sessions, group meetings, training courses, and surveys. The gauge of the OD profession resembles that of therapists: when the client is healthy and doesn't need you any more, you have succeeded. Success sometimes includes working yourself out of a job!

Japan's economic success has stirred tremendous interest in Japanese business and management practices. About ten years ago, U.S. executives began to study their ways and were so impressed, or should I say impressionable, that some of them began wearing kimonos to the office! Since those days, they have become more sophisticated and realize that important principles can be learned from others, but the new users must tailor them to their own circumstances.

Two major themes that have emerged in the past couple of decades are participation and cooperation. That may sound obvious, but there are still major U.S. corporations in which internal strife and competition for promotions dominate day-to-day activities. Human politics will always arise when people work in groups, but when it overrides the needs of the business, failure looms. The team that works together for a common goal will always prevail over a group of individuals pursuing only their own gain and aggrandizement.

In the U.S.A. we are slowly learning to work as teams contributing to company goals. But it is sometimes necessary to change company structure to build a team. Often the simple act of breaking down an old, petrified structure and replacing it with one that enhances communication yields startling results.

The U.S. work force has already transformed itself significantly. Today, customer orientation means accountability not only to customers but also to one's fellow employees.

One secret of OD work is that you don't need a perfect solution. What you need is focus of effort, sincerity of intention, and the stamina to follow through. With those qualities, almost any change will produce gains. The misnomer that a particular problem has only one "perfect" solution can immobilize consultant and company alike. In reality, it is mutual commitment from all those involved in the problem that leads to a solution.

Auto manufacturers have utilized the team concept to improve their manufacturing. The General Motors subsidiary, Saturn Corporation, for example, operates differently from traditional plants. The primary subsets of work in the plant are performed in "business units," sections responsible for output of a complete subunit of the product (rather than just one part of one component). These units now have responsibility for manufacturing indicators once the domain of plant managers. For example, a business unit shows cost, cost savings, profit, and performance on schedule.

Business units are composed of work teams, each of which is responsible for the manufacture of a complete section of the final product. Work teams are subsets of business units. For example, at Saturn, the "Powertrain" business unit constructs the entire engine and transmission. "Powertrain" is also responsible for maintaining costs, meeting schedules, and meeting quality requirements. In effect, it functions as a minifactory within the factory. For work that requires specialization within the business unit, additional teams are created, which, like the larger business units, work together to produce discrete, measurable units of work. These teams might install an entire engine or put in all the glass. Their work is visible to them and to management. They take pride in their work.

By comparison, in a traditional assembly line, a worker's job might be to bolt a manifold onto an engine or to install headlamps. Under such conditions, a worker is unlikely to develop pride of workmanship. It's difficult to feel professional commitment to a string of vehicles that move on a conveyor belt at the speed of one per fifty seconds. At Saturn Corporation, however, workers have autonomy, and genuinely experience pride and ownership in their work.

Companies that incorporate human values into the design of the work environment are much more likely to succeed. When a company demonstrates up front a belief in the value of people, their abilities, and their contributions, workers feel more empathy with company expectations. At Saturn Corporation, people are given meaningful work and the ability to be efficient and produce high-quality products, and the teams highlight the value of cooperation.

Participation is the other key element in company atmosphere. When people know they are valued for their brain power as well as their manual skills, they are truly motivated. Everyone wins in this situation. The company obtains incalculable benefit from people bringing their ideas forward. The individuals who realize that their opinions are welcome feel more interest in their work and their company. In any factory, the most effective managers, engineers, and technicians know how to communicate well with the workers. They know that most of the wisdom about factory operations resides in the workers. This phenomenon was demonstrated by a high-tech company's behavioral analysis of several hundred employees who had been rated as superior by their managers. (The company prefers to remain anonymous.) Their managers were observed communicating with fellow employees more frequently and for longer periods than were their less successful counterparts.

Industrial humanism is the diffusion of humanistic principles into the discipline of management. Terms such as *values, vision, sensitivity,* and *openness* were once used chiefly by humanistic psychologists; now they are finding their way into corporate corridors.

During the 1970s, "growth centers" drew people who wanted to become enlightened about the mysteries of themselves. Those who watched this movement from the outside saw some astonishing sights—dyed-in-the-wool professors sprouting long hair and wearing beads, open displays of affection on the streets, people smiling beatifically.

While psychologists got enlightened, other people got high on drugs. By the 1980s, the Haight-Ashbury age was over. The national mood became more conservative. Professors cut their hair and stopped wearing beads: they needed their jobs. But many ideas that germinated during that period took root.

In the 1980s, as international competition began to subsume increasingly large shares of markets, corporate America became more desperate. The concept of "people power" reemerged in the form of participative work styles, and many of the psychologists of the '70s became ODs of the '80s. Important core values, such as the dignity of the individual and the importance of open communication, had survived. The fads disappeared, but the substance of the humanistic movement remained.

The organizational development movement is reaching new levels of sophistication. OD consultants help with the design of new start-up organizations as well as the transformation of existing ones.

An organizational redesign is well underway at Northern Telecom's semiconductor plant in Rancho Bernardo, California. The factory changed top management in January 1985, and a long-term goal was set to dramatically improve the division's performance, which had seriously deteriorated during 1984.

During the initial stage of reorganization the general manager and his staff of directors began a series of off-site meetings facilitated by an experienced OD. A mini growth center environment was created, at which two- or three-day sessions were held. Participants were exposed to such experiences as values clarification exercises, interpersonal communication techniques, and *visioning,* an exercise in which group members access the intuitive, creative side of themselves to imagine (en*vision)* what an unrestricted, totally successful future for their company would be like. Group members discuss individual visions and work them into a single statement. The statement becomes the navigating star for the rest of their journey.

Group members also confront their own values and level of commitment to those values. One technique used to accomplish this was "what ifs." Participants were confronted with complex scenarios and asked what action they would take under the conditions described. Then the group would analyze responses in comparison with stated values. Powerful emotional experiences were evoked as the group worked on simulations that forced choices between their commitment to people and their obligation to respond to business pressures. They chose to value people. (When this management group later faced real problems that paralleled their simulation exercises, they again had the courage to stand by their people.)

After several months of self-education and development, this group produced a written document of its vision for the future of the plant. The vision provided the focus for all of the activities that followed. The text follows:

> *Innovation*
>
> We have a vision of an environment where change is encouraged and all ideas are heard; where the means to implementation are clear; where recognition and acknowledgment are honest and open, and fear of failure does not exist; where teams replace structure and functional boundaries are broken down; where the vision of the future is shared by everyone.
>
> *Quality*
>
> We have a vision where quality is not a function, but a way of life; where quality in human resources is the same as quality in manufacturing; where quality in our relationships inspires quality in our workplace.
>
> *Human Resources*
>
> We have a vision where the organization promotes human trust, believes in fair practices, recognizes the whole person, provides opportunities for human development; where people work together for a common goal and share in the success of the division; where multicultural differences are cherished and people are responsible for their own behavior; where there is self and

peer assessment; where management is integrated with workers and the manager's main role is to remove barriers and create a communication network.

The next stage was education and buy-in of the vision for about seventy first-level and midlevel managers. These managers were divided into two groups, and each spent a week at off-site sessions. During these meetings, they were exposed to the vision and given the opportunity to visualize and examine their own values as well. Openness was stressed because team building couldn't occur without it. By the end of these sessions, fifteen months had elapsed since the directors began their activities.

The third stage brought the rest of the employees fully into the process. The staff attended a one-day session that introduced them to the vision and helped them understand it. The entire plant now understood the vision and had a copy of a handbook explaining it: the "Human Resources Strategic Document" (HRSD).

From that point on, everyone was expected to try to live up to the standards set in the handbook. In a natural, evolutionary way, as opposed to lock-step enforcement, staff attitudes began to change. Early evidence of the change came in the formation of task teams representing all levels of the organization to design major policy proposals.

More evidence: teams for examining pay practices and attendance policies were empowered to design and present proposals for new policies. Most of their recommendations were implemented. Overall cooperation and openness throughout the facility increased dramatically and became permanent, as could be seen in a hundred ways every day. People behaved with more accountability and respect for one another. It became normal for everyone to come on time to meetings. It became normal to treat any concerns and information brought forward by employees as important. And participatory management became a norm throughout the plant.

The company followed through on the expectations for behavioral change. A considerable amount of one-on-one consulting was conducted by the internal OD group and the outside consultant. One-on-one counseling was arranged to support the people in this commitment to change, at whatever level the organization required it. Because honest confrontation was a stated value in the vision, many one-on-one meetings were held with top managers and initiated by line-level employees. There was also a continual flow of strategically communicated information intended to reinforce the new culture and address problems as they arose. The weekly newsletter carefully and thoroughly explained activities in order to help everyone feel a part of the transition process. Top management regularly attended all major employee meetings to answer questions and show support.

Several changes in key management positions were made to ensure total support of the new culture. Task teams designed not only the job descriptions for key management positions, but selection criteria and procedures as well. As a result, all key management positions below the director's level were posted for internal application. After screening, applicants underwent team interviews, simulations, and technical testing. The new management team included only one former top manager.

Finally, the organization was ready to examine its structure. Fourteen people spent three months off site in uninterrupted study of the manufacturing organization. Group members represented all echelons, from operations director to operators from the plant floor. After extensive study, the group recommended a new structure, which was accepted by the senior management team.

The new structure differed strikingly from the former one. Job areas on the floor were redesigned to put meaning and measurability into the work unit. Functional groups became business units that had goals of quantity, quality, and financial performance. Previously separate groups of operators, engineers, maintenance technicians, quality assurance specialists, and trainers were broken up into teams, with each member contributing different expertise.

Because the new business units differed so much from former divisions, new management jobs were defined and posted. Some people found themselves applying for what resembled their old job. A professional assessment team helped the division create the selection process, leading the way to a thorough and impartial selection of the new management team.

The remaining support groups for manufacturing were restructured during a two-month period in which participation by all affected employees was encouraged. A series of meetings was held over four weeks, and the groups tried to restructure based on criteria from the general manager: to avoid duplication, to locate for maximum communication, and to have logical reasoning behind the proposals.

The reorganization created a huge demand for training and cross training. One intention of the new vision was to enrich the workers' jobs by giving them a much wider range of work assignments. For example, if a person's sole responsibility under the old structure had been to operate a single machine, under the new structure, he or she would learn how to maintain it. Where before people might have been recording numbers without knowing the reason for it, afterward they got the chance to learn why.

In addition to technical training, skill building in the areas of teamwork, leadership, employee development, and communication were in great demand. The level of commitment to the vision of providing needed resources for everyone was so high that training activities became a part of almost everyone's job.

During these organizational changes, Northern Telecom at Rancho Bernardo experienced a downturn in business. In line with its commitment to people, no one was laid off. Rather than choosing the easy but shortsighted solution of a layoff, the management affirmed its belief in people and their skills by retraining workers on a temporary basis for other jobs. This strategy preserved the trained labor force and resulted in high performance later, when business picked up again.

The management at Rancho Bernardo made a major investment in the future with a clarity of vision and a dedication to quality and humanistic values. The general manager made a bold commitment and stuck tenaciously to it. He played a critical role by communicating with the rest of the corporation, effectively protecting the experiment, and giving it time to flower. As of this writing, the process is three years old and, in the opinion of the staff and ODs, the impact of the change is probably just beginning to be realized. At this interim stage, however, all of the key manufacturing indicators have shown a positive trend over a two-year period. Factory yields have reached an all-time high and are competitive by industry standards. Indications suggest continued progress in that important area.

As a division of a vastly larger multinational corporation, the population of the plant represents less than 1 percent of the corporation. Although Rancho Bernardo continues to improve upon its already high-quality performance, the long-range future of the plant will ultimately be decided by factors significantly within its control. For example, decisions made by corporate management will include a supplier strategy that looks to its own inhouse capabilities first and operates from a knowledge of proven value added. In keeping with their proactive philosophies, managers are not taking a wait-and-see attitude. Instead, they are aggressively and vigorously exploring ways to develop expertise and capabilities to meet the future needs of the corporation. The plant's management is not only demonstrating performance that encourages increasing support from Northern Telecom headquarters but is also providing a leadership role model for the rest of the corporation by reorganizing to meet the challenges of the future. In keeping with the flexible and proactive nature of the new organization, managers are aggressively pursuing opportunities for technological leadership that make them indispensable to the parent company.

Industrial humanism is not about total security. It is about creating high-quality products, being constructively competitive in world business, and having a sense of satisfaction and pride in one's job. Industrial humanism is a phenomenon whose time has come, and it is a philosophy that will grow as long as it contributes to success in the market place.

For the United States, this philosophy is essential. Workers who have teamwork skills, an orientation to quality, a strong work ethic, and the ability to participate in decision making can make significant contributions to any industry.

11

The American Dream

In 1776, when Paul Revere waited for the signal of "one if by land, two if by sea," he understood exactly what was happening. The fledgling United States of America was under attack. When he rode with word of the impending invasion, everyone understood and rallied together. In those far simpler times, Americans made a choice to fight for freedom and democracy.

In the next 200 years, the United States grew to become a superpower. Today, few issues seem clear and simple. However, some things are obvious. Living in America is the dream of millions of oppressed people around the world. Many pin their hopes for themselves or their children on a life in this country. For both citizens and refugees, there is still an American Dream. For some refugees, it represents escape from inhumanity, persecution, and starvation; for others, economic opportunity on a scale unavailable in their homelands. For citizens of this country, the interpretation of the dream varies among individuals. My interpretation will set the tone for the rest of this chapter.

First and foremost, the American Dream is the grand and noble experiment called democracy. The freedoms and liberties guaranteed by our Constitution inspire oppressed people around the world. Social critics have the freedom to point out glaring imperfections in how we implement democracy. That is one of our strengths. The fact that our society is the source of hopes and dreams of many people living under totalitarian governments makes us a permanent threat to those systems.

Second, the American Dream represents a high standard of living. Business, educational, and personal opportunities are unparalleled. This component of the American Dream is driven by financial factors, such as a growing economy and a stable, reasonable balance of trade.

I would like to believe that our commitment to democratic values is as deep as that of our forefathers. I would like to believe that, regardless of economics, we, as a nation of individuals, would never compromise our values. However, our 200 years as a nation has been a time of evolution. The standard of living we now enjoy is inextricably woven into our national consciousness and our conception of democracy. The protection and nurturance of our industrial base is strategically important to the defense of this country. In my mind, our economic competition is just as critical as our military maneuvering.

Once again, I will use Japan as an example. A country that was in ruins only forty years ago has risen to a position of power and influence. It did not accomplish this by rebuilding its armed forces to compel the respect of other countries. It achieved the feat through economics. Japanese citizens now own land in countries all around the world. They manage resources and people on a global scale, and they do not require military force to maintain their expanding influence. Remember that their competitive strategy is to approach the market place as if to prepare for battle. The Japanese have used military principles and ethics to achieve economic victory. They have, in effect, accomplished one of the basic purposes of most wars: to control people and resources.

Japan's limiting of expenditures for rebuilding its military was originally a condition imposed when it surrendered at the end of World War II. However, that limited military spending, combined with massive American financial and technological assistance, created fertile conditions for economic growth. After a brief adjustment period, Japan recognized its opportunity and created long-range plans to capitalize on it. Today Japan spends approximately 1 percent of its gross national product on defense. By comparison, the U.S. spends about 6 percent. (The comparison is similar with almost all of our nation's strategic allies, such as West Germany.) Saving on military spending provides Japan and other countries with ongoing leverage to invest lavishly in research and development projects. This strategy gives them the ability to move quickly in developing new manufacturing technologies and new products.

Key to their success has been a reputation for high-quality products and penetration into growth markets, especially high-technology components.

The most visible result of Japan's success is its amazingly favorable trade balance. The Japanese make a lot of money in their business dealings. More important, however, they have created tremendous growth in the opportunities for their people. They are one of the most literate countries in the world. A Japanese child receives some of the best education anywhere.

Many Japanese auto makers have established factories in the United States. This creates jobs for U.S. workers. However, the bad news is missing components! We may build the cars, but Japan manufactures the most sophisticated electronic and mechanical parts and ship them here. The profit Japan reaps from a few small packages shipped to its U.S. subsidiaries often exceeds the entire profit the factory makes from the rest of the car.

There is a natural evolution in national economics. When advanced countries improve the standard of living for their citizens, it causes higher salary expectations. Eventually, advanced nations (such as the United States, Japan, England, France, and West Germany) price themselves out of the lower-end labor markets. The need for cheap labor causes jobs to migrate to developing nations. Textile work, for example, has migrated from the U.S.A. to Japan, to Korea, then to Sri Lanka, and so on. Advanced nations must capitalize on their technological prowess and fight among themselves to retain the lead in critical fields.

Many U.S. multinational corporations show financial growth and significant profit. However, they often use tactics that, in the long run, undermine our nation's economy. In their quest for cheaper labor and more favorable tax conditions, many U.S. companies are moving their manufacturing operation out of the country. The result is fancy headquarters in Chicago, New York, and Los Angeles, but the rest of the company, the jobs, the research opportunities, the chance for U.S. workers to develop skills, are gone. Despite appearances, the truth is that many companies have just packed up and left.

What will bring the jobs back? How can we prevent further erosion of the U.S. work force? There is no simple answer. Perhaps we can control trade or require a certain percentage of domestic labor content. The ramifications of many of the economic proposals are extremely complex. Perhaps some good simulation work on the subject would help.

At any rate, it's clear that U.S. companies are competing under a handicap. In most other countries, government cooperation with and assistance to high-tech companies provides them with considerable leverage. The government of any industrialized country makes a formidable competitor for any U.S. company. In some countries, such as Japan, the government actually gets involved in establishing quality standards and certifying workers. Regardless of how distasteful that sounds to us, we cannot ignore the results.

The government has a major responsibility to plan and develop the correct response to this problem. I applaud the efforts of National Semiconductor chairman Al Sporock to involve the government in a consortium of semiconductor manufacturers (SEMTECH) to design the world's most advanced semiconductor manufacturing system. It is most assuredly a step in the right direction.

Another strategy is to create a long-term plan to increase the capability of the U.S. worker. The result would be a worldwide perception of the U.S. worker as a quality-driven craftsperson. Quality workmanship can play a significant role in regaining the prestige we have lost.

Who might the players be in a strategy of this kind? Industry, government, and education working together under the right conditions could do the job. The role of education would be to pursue its current plans to repair the weaknesses of the nation's schools. The role of industry would be to improve its customer orientation and stand firm on quality standards.

Government, in this scheme, plays the most radical role. The government must take steps to encourage the upgrading of the American worker. Programs such as the Job Training Partnership Act (JTPA) are useful for the purposes for which they were designed. JTPA basically funds training for displaced workers and workers who are difficult to employ, and retraining for workers who would otherwise be displaced by their employers. Private industry councils are a fine vehicle for ensuring that the administration of funds is in line with real industry needs.

The government should provide strong encouragement for research and development in the private sector. Tax exemptions should be generous. The same goes for training and development. Funding for research and training is funding for the future.

But the area in which the government has the most power to influence how business is done in the United States is taxation. A purist would argue that the tax system should not be used to prescribe action: it should stick to collecting taxes. However, that is not how things work. An activity that is deductible from a business tax base is an activity a business will find a way to do. If some arrangements were made granting tax benefits for employee inhouse training, companies would find a way to do it.

I am not in any sense suggesting a give-away. Earlier, I suggested proactive action, implying the creation of *conditions that would encourage* industry to be thorough and conscientious in providing training and education for employees. For example, the government could offer a national certification in manufacturing. It need not be a requirement in any sense (including eligibility for government contracts), but a way to escalate the visibility of worker accomplishments and to determine whether the tax deduction for training is warranted.

Another approach might be to find ways to reward companies having a viable strategy for the training and development of their people. If the company business plan contained details of the allocation of resources for the training of its employees, and if the company delivered training that met standards, it could receive tax deductions.

One way or another, government must tackle this problem of the eroding U.S. work force. In the long run, this step is as essential to preserving peace as building a strong military. It is only the size of our industrial base that keeps the true extent of the crisis from standing out in bold relief. Our foundations are crumbling, and the speed of decline could increase.

As mentioned in chapter 5, the Japanese approach to business essentially involves warfare strategy. This must be understood in its historical context. When one group in a nation or world raises the ante and operates outside of the currently accepted framework, it usually signals the dawn of a new era.

In the arena of warfare, the principle is obvious. In the early 1800s, Shaka became chief of the Zulus. African warfare, up until his time, had consisted mostly of threats—noise, gesturing, and relatively minor physical confrontation. Death from warfare was rare. Shaka, however, developed lethal tactics and strategies, and conditioned his warriors through extremely rigorous training. When his men entered a battlefield of noisemakers and gesturers, slaughter ensued. From that point on, there was a new era and no turning back. Every nation in Africa adopted lethal warfare tactics.

We can respond to Japan's competitive edge in economics in any number of ways. Congress can pass trade legislation and tariffs. We can write lengthy editorials about how predatory Japanese practices are. We can launch "Buy American" campaigns. But whatever our responses, we had better understand that a new era has begun. Japan has upped the ante in the world trade stakes, and there is no going back.

Our nation is large enough to do some muscle flexing and has forced Japan into modifying its trading practices. But our size is only a buffer, not a defense. We will not be devastated by the first assault, but we have only a limited time to realize that our industries must work harder, be more customer oriented, and produce superior-quality goods and services if the American economy is to survive in the future.

All of us must do our part to stimulate better-quality skills among our workers. Training, particularly technical training, plays an instrumental role in securing our future and preserving the American Dream.

References

Anderson. R. (1983). *Selecting and Developing Media for Instruction*. New York: Van Nostrand Reinhold.

Baldwin, L. (1985). "The National Technological University." In *1986 World Conference on Continuing Engineering Education* (below).

Bennett, W. (1986). *What Works*. Washington, DC: U.S. Department of Education.

Bayes, J. "Electronic Polling: The Teletraining Applications." In Parker and Olgren, *Teleconferencing and Electronic Communications V: Applications, Technologies and Human Factors* (below).

Block, P. (1981). *Flawless Consulting*. San Diego: University Associates.

Bloom. B., Ed. (1977). *Taxonomy of Educational Objectives*, Handbook 1. New York: Longman.

Capell, J., et al. "An Industry/Education Partnership in Santa Clara County." In *Teleconferencing and Electronic Communications (below).*

Corporation for Public Broadcasting. (1986). Instructional Technology in Higher Education: A National Study of the Educational Uses of Technology in America's Colleges and Universities. Washington, DC: CPB.

Crosby, J. *Data Based Training*. Phoenix, AZ: Crosby.

DeMont, M. (1986). "Teleconferencing: A Primer." In *Teleconferencing and Electronic Communications V* (below).

Dick, W. and Carey, L. (1985). *The Systematic Design of Instruction*. New York: Scott Foresman.

Deutsch, R. (1987). *Nuclear Power*. Columbia, MD: GP Courseware.

Grayson, L., Ed. (1986). *1986 World Conference on Continuing Engineering Education: Proceedings*. Vols. I and II. New York: IEEE Education Society.

Kearsley, G. (1984). *Training and Technology*. New York: Addison-Wesley.

Krathwohl, D., Ed. (1969). Taxonomy of Educational Objectives, Handbook 2. New York: Longman.

Mager, R. (1962). *Preparing Instructional Objectives*. Belmont, CA: Pitman Learning.

Moye, A. (1986). "Continuing Education at Hewlett Packard." In *1986 World Conference on Continuing Engineering Education* (above).

O'Neil, H. (1979). Learning Strategies. New York: Academic Press.

Parker, L. and Olgren, C., Eds. (1986). *Teleconferencing and Electronic Communications V: Applications, Technologies and Human Factors*. Madison: University of Wisconsin-Extension.

Payer, D. *Maintenance Training for Reduction of Unscheduled Down Time*. Cupertino, CA: Payer.

Phillips, D. (1986). "The Pennsylvania State Telecommunications and Teleconferencing System." In *Teleconferencing and Electronic Communications V* (above).

Schonberger, R. (1986). "Training: The Catalyst." In *World Class Manufacturing*. New York: The Free Press.

Tsias, S. and Marena, N. (1983). "Introduction to Shuttle Mission Simulations." NASA.

————. (1988) Astronaut Selection and Training. NASA facts, KSC-35-81.

Truesdale, S. (1986). "The Making of a Full Motion Videoconferencing System: Lessons Learned." In *Teleconferencing* (above).

U.S. Nuclear Regulatory Commission. (1980). *Three Mile Island: A Report to the Commissioners and the People*. Washington, DC: Government Printing Office.

Appendix
Gathering Information for the Key Elements of the Business Plan

From Crosy, J. (1985). *Data Based Training*. Phoenix, AZ (self-published). Reprinted with permission.

1. *Statement of your company and what distinguishes it from other companies in the field.*
- Ask around for the names of the employees who have been with the company for a long time. Talk with them and ask them about the early history, how the company was organized, who the founders were, and what their philosophy was.
- If you're a public company, obtain copies of current and previous years' annual reports. Go to the library and check in a Dun & Bradstreet and Standard and Poor's.
- Talk to some of the older salesmen about the earlier products, the competition, and your share of the market.
- Talk to the president or CEO and ask about the operating philosophy of the company. Ask about quality. Ask about growth, profitability, international competition, government control, etc.
- Think about how training can influence or be influenced by these data.

2. *Information about the industry of which your company is a part.*
- Seek out trade associations and ask for information on the history of the industry. Examples would be SEMI, AEA, and IEEE.

■ Contact major stock brokerage firms and ask if they have a market analyst that follows your industry.

■ Check newspapers and magazines for trend information. Read special feature articles that identify significant events or describe new technologies.

■ Integrate this information with the specific company data gathered. Do the two elements change, diverge, or run parallel? What do you see happening in your company that you don't see happening in the industry? Are the differences potentially positive or negative?

■ Think abut how training can influence or be influenced by these data.

3. *Management team and organization structure.*

■ Who are the key players? What are their backgrounds? If no published data are available, stop by and interview them. Note: Do NOT ask them to comment about the others.

■ Ask them questions about your products, the market place, the factory, etc.

■ Ask them what they see as the major challenges facing the organization in the next 3 to 6 months, 6 months to 1 year, and beyond a year.

■ Ask them how their organizational structure helps them achieve the goals of the company.

■ Ask what sort of reports they use to help them manage the business. Ask why they use the particular reports they do.

■ Ask them for their views and expectations of training. Listen carefully and take notes.

■ Think about how training can influence or be influenced by these data.

4. *Product/service provided by your company.*

■ Ask the marketing people to identify your company's major products or services. Do they have the products categorized by application? Do they have them categorized by customer? How are the products organized? What is the purpose of the organization?

■ Talk with the sales and marketing people. Ask them about the benefits of your products. Ask them about the features of the product. How do the features relate to the benefits?

■ Ask about quality. For what reasons do the customers like or dislike your products?

■ Who are your major competitors? What are their strengths and weaknesses? How do their plants operate?

■ Ask where your product is in terms of its life cycle.

■ Think about how training can influence or be influenced by these data.

5. *Market segment served by your company.*

■ Talk with sales and marketing people and ask them to describe or define the segment of the overall market your company serves. For example, a market segment would be disk drives while the overall market would be computer peripherals.

■ Ask what factors influence the segment served by your company. Is the segment growing or shrinking? How may competitors are there? What do we know about their products?

■ Ask about your share of market. Ask how it is determined. Ask what your company's plans are for increasing/decreasing share of market.

■ Ask the sales and marketing people to share their market research and analysis data with you. Review them and make notes.

■ Think about how training can influence or be influenced by these data.

6. *Total market place.*

■ Talk with sales and marketing people and ask about the size of the total market place. What percent is the segment you serve? Is the overall market shrinking or expanding? What factors can you identify that seem to be driving the market?

■ What national or international factors seem to influence the total market? What is the lead/lag relationship between the economy and your market place?
■ What are the major societal trends that have the potential of influencing your market? For example, with the shift from an industrial to an information society, will this increase or decrease your market? Why?
■ Who are the companies that dominate the market? What do you know about them and about their products?
■ Think about how training can influence or be influenced by these data.

7. *Sales and marketing plan.*
■ Ask the sales and marketing people to describe to you how they develop specific activities to make the sales projections. Do they target key clients? Do they advertise? How did they select the mode of advertising?
■ Ask what the specific sales strategy is to sell your company's products to the top five or ten customers.
■ Ask what level of quality has to be in place for each major customer. Do these requirements jibe with how the factory operates? If you don't know, how can you find out?
■ Ask what lead times are being quoted vs. being requested. Does your factory operate inside or outside of the lead times? Why?
■ How do the sales and marketing plans compare with the capacity of your factory? If you don't know, how can you find out?
■ Think about how training can influence or be influenced by these data.

8. *Operations plan.*
■ Meeting with the production manager, manufacturing manager director of operations, VP of operations, or whoever has primary responsibility for operations. Ask about capacities. Ask about cycle times. Ask about production control. Ask about maintenance. Ask about turnover. Ask about training.

■ Ask how operations are organized. Are they organized functionally? Along product lines? Along division lines? Why?
■ What types of reports or information does operations use to help it manage its function? What historical trends are there? How do the trends relate to: (a) the sales forecast, (b) the market segment forecast, (c) the industry, (d) the competition?
■ Ask if the operations group has a manpower forecast. How was it determined? What assumptions for productivity were made? How realistic are they?
■ What about quality? Are there specifications written and in place? Are they being followed? How do you know?
■ Think about how training can influence or be influenced by these data.

9. *R&D plan.*
■ Ask the key members of management, i.e., president or CEO, what types of R&D requirements they see as necessary or desirable.
■ Use the information from sales and marketing, i.e., the product life cycle, to confirm top management's views.
■ How does your information about the major competitors and products compare with the trends in the market place?
■ Does your organization require R&D efforts for products or processes or both?
■ How old are your processes? Your equipment? Your products? Talk with the key engineering people. Ask them what R&D projects are active and why they are active.
■ Will the new products or processes being developed require significantly different people? How can you anticipate this need?
■ What types of resources are needed internally to deliver the R&D effort? People? How can they be prepared?
■ Think about how training can influence or be influenced by these data.

10. *Critical risks.*
■ Are there key people that the organization depends on to

achieve the goals of the business? How can those people be backed up?

- What key processes or pieces of equipment run the risk of shutting you down if they are inoperative? How can this risk be minimized?
- What provisions are there to cross-train key employees?
- What do the key managers see as the major or critical risks to the business?
- How can you/they evaluate those risks? What contingency plans can be put in place to minimize or eliminate the risks?
- Think about how training can influence or be influenced by these data.

11. *Pro forma financials.*

- Pro forma means provided in advance. Pro forma financials are financial projects.
- Get a copy of the operating budget. If algorithms were used to develop the numbers, find out what was used and go through the budget with a fine-tooth comb. Do the numbers square? If not, why not? What opportunities are there for cost reduction?
- Ask the finance people for a variance report or a profit and loss or income statement forecast. Ask what factors went into the generation of the forecast. Do the assumptions check with what others are saying?
- Typically, an income statement forecast will make some assumptions regarding yield and productivity improvements. It is very important that you understand these assumptions and be able to place them in perspective.
- The balance sheet gives you the position of the company's assets and liabilities at a given period of time. You can have less of a direct impact on the balance sheet than on the earnings or income statement.
- The sales and earnings forecast can tell you the sales and earnings expected by month, by quarter, by year, etc. Ask what assumptions went into the development of the forecast.

Do the sales and revenue ranges coincide with what you're being asked to do? If not, why not?

■ Think about how training can influence or be influenced by these data.

12. *Appendices.*

■ Include all notes, assumptions, surveys, etc. that were used to generate the business plan or were used in your data-gathering process.